Praise for The Walk of a Lifetime

Books on the pilgrimage to Santiago de Compostela are many, but few capture the richness of the experience as well as Russ Eanes' *The Walk of a Lifetime*. It merits a slow reading so that its spiritual and human truths might be deeply savored.

—Kevin Codd, author of *To the Field of Stars: A Pilgrim's Journey to Santiago de Compostela*

What sets *Walk of a Lifetime* apart from the many hundreds of other Camino books is the clarity of the writing, the vivid descriptions and the author's sheer sincerity which shines through as he narrates his journey along the Camino Francés. I enjoyed reading this book. You will too.

—Johnnie Walker, author of *It's About Time: A Call to the Camino de Santiago* and numerous Camino guidebooks

Russ Eanes has created a lovely travelogue that is blessedly bathed in his prayerful, positive and cheerful outlook... a transformative experience... a joy to each footstep.

Sandy Brown, pilgrim guide and Camino guidebook author

THE WALK OF A LIFETIME

500 Miles on the Camino de Santiago

RUSS EANES

The Walker Press

The Walker Press

www.thewalkerpress.com

ISBN Softcover: 978-1-7333036-0-6

This book is a memoir, reflecting the author's recollection of actual experiences. Some events are combined and some names have been changed where the author felt it best to respect an individual's privacy.

All scripture quotations are from the New International Version of the Bible, unless otherwise noted.

www.thewalkerpress.com

Author bio photo courtesy of Kate Bennet. All other photos by the author.

Map of the Camino Routes of Europe courtesy of WalkFarMedia.com, ©Jean Christie Ashmore from *Camino de Santiago: To Walk Far, Carry Less*

Map of Camino Frances at the back of the book is from the WikiMedia Commons

Cover design by Nathan Eanes and Merrill Miller

*To my wife Jane, who encouraged
and blessed this journey;
And who walked by my side
as I entered Santiago.*

Also by Russ Eanes

Pilgrim Paths to Assisi: 300 Miles on the Way of St. Francis

Contents

Part V

Arriving

Foreword

The next time you hear someone announce the final demise of God or Christianity or religion – take your pick – recommend they take a walk on the *Camino de Santiago*. If they can't do that for some reason, then give them this wonderful book.

The *Camino* is a mystical magnet for many people around the world. In the 1970s, a few dozen people annually walked the route as pilgrims. In the late 1980s, the figure rose to a couple of thousand or so. By the mid-1990s, there were 25,000, a tenfold increase, and by 2005 (the first time I went) there were almost 100,000. The year Russ walked it, over 300,000 people officially registered as pilgrims completing the journey.

Churchgoing is declining, especially in Europe, but pilgrimage is increasing there and elsewhere. God is not dead, but meeting people on the road. That is why Russ – like many people, including me – believes that a *Camino* pilgrimage can be life changing. He and I and so many others found it so.

But why?

The *Camino* pilgrimage can be a complex retreat experience that contrasts with daily life and suggests ways to live differently.

First, this pilgrimage is demanding. One uproots from home – taking time off work, from family, or other commitments – and goes to a distant place. Then one moves slowly and in physically demanding ways over a great span, walking (or cycling) farther on a daily basis than most North Americans do in a week or even a month. One is left alone with one's thoughts and fears, but still persists. This is in contrast to our normal push button, touch screen reality where we expect conveniences to be instantly available and at our command. On the *Camino*, we learn and achieve only very slowly; I like to call it the speed of life.

Second, ironically, we undertake the *Camino* in a form of solitude, but end up being widely and richly connected: with pilgrims from around the world that we meet and care for and are supported by; with nature and weather that we encounter directly by being outside; with faithful people who journeyed before us; with those who give hospitality along the way; with long standing Christian traditions and history. This is in contrast to the thin, self-selecting isolation where many of us focus exclusively on our devices – even on dates in restaurants, even while walking with our children on the street.

Third, the *Camino* reorients us. It teaches us true priorities about hospitality and sharing, about listening to the Spirit and caring for strangers, about a healthy pace of life, and trusting in God's providence. This in contrast to an urgent world that pummels us with so many demands that we often are not even sure what we truly believe or want to do.

Don't take my word for it. Russ testifies to the same realities. If he or I tell you to take a hike, we are not insulting you, we are trying to do you a favor.

Arthur Boers
Author of *The Way is Made by Walking: A Pilgrimage Along the Camino de Santiago*

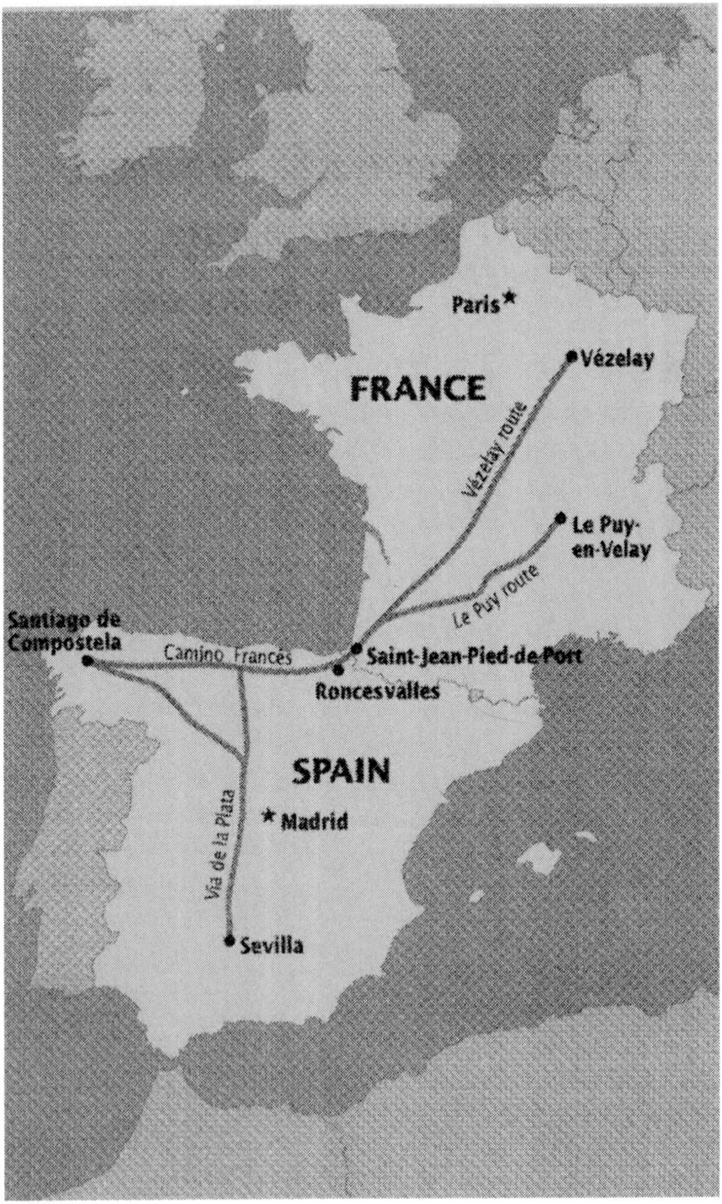
Paris
Vézelay
FRANCE
Vézelay route
Le Puy-
en-Velay
Le Puy route
Santiago de
Compostela
Camino Francés
Saint-Jean-Pied-de-Port
Roncesvalles
SPAIN
Madrid
Via de la Plata
Sevilla

Map of the Camino Frances

PART I

Departing

Whispers of the Camino

When you plan a journey,
  It belongs to you.
When you begin a journey,
  You belong to it.

African Proverb

I PAUSED as I stepped over the threshold of my back door, keenly aware that with that step a long-awaited pilgrimage was beginning. I was leaving for Spain for six weeks. It was a journey I'd been dreaming of for two decades, but it was also the longest time I had been away from my home and family in 39 years. The trees in the woods behind my house were still bare. The grass on the back slope was brown; small patches of melting snow lay on the edges near the woods.

My flight would take off in about six hours. I had wanted to walk across town to catch the airport bus that morning—I was about to walk 500 miles, so the three miles didn't seem like much—but freezing rain was falling and my wife Jane insisted on driving me. I hate farewells and was pulled in two directions: eager to get going, but resisting the moment I would have to say goodbye. It was only a little over four weeks until she would join me, but that's a long time when someone has been part of your every day, every decision, in some ways every breath, for nearly 40 years. The drive took ten minutes. Because it was raining hard and because the bus was about to leave, we only had time for a brief hug and a quick kiss. I hopped out of the car, reached into the back and grabbed my pack and poles. I sloshed through a few deep puddles and boarded the bus. The driver glared at me impatiently, since I was the last person to board, but just then my oldest son and grandson ran up and I jumped out to give them a final hug, too.

I had been waiting for this moment for years, had been preparing for it for months, but suddenly the thought of putting an ocean between me and everyone I loved, for so long, seemed momentous. My eyes swelled with tears as I sank into my seat and waved farewell to them all one more time through the bus window.

THE CAMINO DE SANTIAGO had been whispering to me for nearly 20 years. I first read of it in a medieval autobiography—the *Book of Margery Kempe*—an early 14th century English mystic, who took several pilgrimages herself, to Rome, the Holy Land and to Santiago de Compostela.[1] I was intrigued by its history and its mystical draw on people. At its peak—in the 12th through 14th centuries, perhaps up to a half a million people walked to and from Santiago, believed to be the burial place of the Apostle James. Many sought a miracle; some were doing penance. Others simply craved adventure and to see something beyond their own town or village, since the average person in the Middle Ages rarely traveled more than a few kilometers away from home.

I learned that medieval Europe was ripe with pilgrimages,[2] and Santiago, after Rome and Jerusalem, was the most popular destination; in the 13th and 14th centuries it even exceeded those two. In northern Spain during the Middle Ages, whole towns and villages grew up to support it. The path provided for significant cultural exchange between northern Spain and the rest of Europe; the German poet Goethe is quoted saying, "Europe was made on the Pilgrim Road to Compostela." The round-trip for those walking from the far reaches of France or Germany would be more than 2,000 miles, or 3,200 kilometers. The entire journey might take them years and many died along the way. Never a single route, the Camino was a network of roads, snaking across France and Spain, at points merging and then separating. But from France and beyond, as they reached the Spanish border, most converged in or near the town St.-Jean-Pied-de-Port in the French Pyrenees, and from there on the most popular route—and the most famous— became known as the *Camino Frances*, or the "French Way." From there to Santiago it is 500 miles or 800 kilometers.[3] Previous routes, especially along the Northern Coast had existed for centuries, but the Camino Frances proved to be the easiest to traverse. Guidebooks were written for would-be pilgrims.[4] Some went on horseback, but most went on foot, typically carrying a small bag for food, a staff, a jug or gourd for water and a hat to fend off the bright Spanish sun. They had to contend with thieves, con-men, swollen rivers, heavy snowfall, rain, freezing winds, scorching heat, and the endless, wide-open and occasionally disorienting *Meseta* (or Spanish Plain). Churches and monasteries founded *hospitals*, or places of hospitality, providing free food, lodging and care for the sick. Fountains were built in the town squares for quenching pilgrims' thirst. *Peregrinos*,[5] as they were known, often walked in groups for safety, stopping to view magnificent churches and Cathedrals, many of which still exist. The Way[6] followed an old Roman road, which itself may have followed a still more ancient route from Celtic and pre-Celtic times.[7]

The Camino experienced a slow decline in the 16th and 17th centuries after the Protestant Reformation. By the 18th century, the flood of pilgrims slowed to a trickle, though it never ceased entirely, and many of the smaller towns and villages fell into ruin. But the memory of its greatness and its mystical intrigue never completely left the people who lived along it or the imaginations of those who heard about it.

The modern revival of the Camino began about 40 years ago, largely through the work of a Spanish priest, Father Elias Valiña Sampredo, who conceived of the route marked with yellow arrows. Today it is a major Cultural Itinerary of Europe and UNESCO has declared it a World Heritage Site. Since parts of the old *Calzada*,[8] the original route (and Roman road), was then and still is under the asphalt of highways, alternative dirt paths have been created, sometimes going alongside the modern highways, though long stretches of the old dirt road still make up much of the Camino Frances. The ancient Camino towns came back to life; the ruined and depopulated villages were gradually rebuilt. Hostels—called *refugios or albergues*[9]— along with hotels, grocers, cafés and restaurants, were opened. Modern pilgrims can find a place to eat or sleep every few kilometers along its entire length and a bed in an albergue can cost as little as €5 (or $6.) Those on a tight budget can manage easily for as little as €30 /day and reservations for lodging are not required. From a trickle in the 1980s, the Way has again experienced a surge, with more than 300,000 pilgrims walking all or part of it annually, as in the Middle Ages.[10]

For a decade I read about the Way, or met people who had been on it. The whisper grew louder. Ten years ago, the author and friend, Arthur Paul Boers, handed me a copy of his book, *The Way is Made by Walking*, a memoir of his pilgrimage. I quickly devoured it and became determined that I would walk it the first chance I had. The whisper became a calling, a dream. But when would I do it? With the responsibilities of a husband and father, taking six weeks off to walk the Camino Frances was not an option. Friends suggested I do it in parts or stages, maybe two weeks at a time. Some suggested cycling it, which would take less than half the time. But this wasn't just a "bucket list" item, a box to check off labeled "Camino." I wanted a life-changing experience—something restorative—and that was only going to happen step-by-step, over time. I needed to do the whole thing in *one go*. I didn't know that I would wait another ten years for the chance.

I HAVE ALWAYS HAD an adventurous spirit. The youngest in a family of four baby-boomers, I grew up on the edges of suburbs in both Pennsylvania and Connecticut. I played in the streets or ran in the woods while traveling deep in my imagination. Back then, play dates didn't exist, phones were attached to the wall, there were just three TV channels and they only played reruns in the afternoons after school—and that drove me out of the house. When I wasn't outside, I devoured books, collected postage stamps and dreamed of traveling the globe as a writer. I had a large map of the world on my bedroom wall, which I studied in detail. I routinely fell asleep with an encyclopedia on the bed, its pages open to some obscure country of the world.

Meanwhile the upheaval of the 1960s was happening around me and I was aware of it all: the civil rights and environmental movements, the sexual revolution, the war in Vietnam and later, women's liberation and Watergate. My dad may have been in the Army when we were all born, but by the end of the decade my older brothers were demonstrating against the war and going to Woodstock. They were ten years older than me and as an adolescent I laid awake during the hot, sticky summer nights, the sounds of Bob Dylan and Joan Baez drifting in from their room next door. Everything in society seemed up for questioning and I questioned it all. We were middle-class, but my social conscience was stirred and I grew up to become a nonconformist, as well as adventurous.

I began college eager to become a writer, a journalist, but by the first year I was aimless and partying. At the end of my second year, I was introduced to Christianity; my social consciousness was reinforced deeply by the teachings of Jesus in the Gospels, but I couldn't fit into the conservative groove of contemporary American Evangelicalism. I went to seminary after college, intent on pursuing a career as a traditional pastor, but that didn't fit either. After I met and married Jane, we decided to follow the most committed spiritual path we could. We moved into an intentional Christian community where no one owned anything; everything was shared among the community members, and with the poor. The dream lasted nearly two decades, until the time came to move on. We relocated across the country, to help care for my ailing parents. Starting over was not easy: we left the community with six children, few material possessions and no bank account. We struggled financially, but it drew our family closer.

Over the next years we built a new life: I began work full-time at a state university and went to school in the evenings to obtain a Master's degree. Family continued to be the most important thing about my life and I tried to keep that a priority, even with a demanding career. At age 49 I became a grandfather and our already large family began to expand as our children married. I eventually went back into ministry, where I managed to couple my spiritual calling with my love of writing, working for the publishing house of a major Christian denomination, the last seven years as its executive director. In that role we came to the Shenandoah Valley where we sank our roots—growing fruits and vegetables on an acre of land, surrounded again by the woods. We ride our bikes to the farmer's market and eat supper on our front deck on summer evenings, watching the sun set over the mountains.

In recent years I traveled across the U.S., some of it personal, but much of it for work. It wasn't until we were in our early fifties that my wife and I were able to fulfill the dream fueled so long ago by that map of the world in my childhood bedroom. In the course of a decade we went twice to South America and several times to Europe, visiting the UK, Ireland, France, Germany and Switzerland. We hiked the Cliffs of Moher, the Scottish Borders, Hadrian's Wall, the Rhine Valley, the vineyards of Alsace, the Swiss Alps. In Vézelay, France, a common collection point in France for medieval pilgrims, I bought a map of Europe showing all the Camino routes to Santiago and put it on my wall, a source of inspiration. Yet all this hiking was only a rehearsal for *the* Camino, which remained my dream. As time went by, the idea that I would walk the entire Camino Frances took mythical proportions in my mind, rehearsing in my imagination the arrival and start of the pilgrimage in the medieval city of St.-Jean. Like the characters in the movie "Close Encounters," I felt as if I had been imprinted, was being called, chosen, and I could not explain it.

I have been fortunate enough to work in jobs where I could serve a higher purpose and I mostly loved my work. Yet, there was no escaping the boxed-in world of contemporary American society. My time became parsed into the days of the weeks, the hours of the day, the appointments on my calendar and the items on my to-do list. I shouldered priorities that weren't my own; I had to play roles to do my job. There were budgets that continually shrank, constituencies that disagreed; the publishing industry went through tremendous and disheartening disruption. I became an expert at down-sizing a business, but over time this wears a person down. I was at the pinnacle of my career, but it was time for a change. I had been convinced for decades that the pace of my life—along with most Americans—was too fast, too busy, and that I needed more time and space to appreciate what was going on around me, to listen more deeply to God through the "everyday."

My opportunity came this past year, not long after I decided to leave my job and take my own year-long, unpaid sabbatical. I had reached 60 and knew it was the time. My last child had graduated from high school and the nest was officially empty. I was too young to retire, but old enough to know that I needed to slow down and reorient my life. My dream had grown: besides going on a pilgrimage, I wanted to take an entire year to re-set my life—to pause, to "downshift," to start living in a slower gear. I left my job the first week in January, allowing myself three months to prepare.

As a road cyclist, I routinely biked over 3,000 kilometers (2,000 miles) per year, but I wanted to be in better shape, so I took regular fitness classes and began to build new strength and lose weight. A few weeks before I left I walked longer and longer distances, gradually building up to 25 kilometers (15 miles) per day with a full pack. I bought guidebooks and digested them, selecting one to take along with me. I watched YouTube videos and read online forums. I collected my equipment, carefully selecting and weighing my pack's contents down to the gram.

In addition to physically conditioning my body, I prepared my spirit for the journey, thinking through my rationale and creating guiding principles. When asked about what I intended to do while I walked, I replied, "think, pray, talk to strangers, make new friends and see what opens up for me each day." I developed these simple rules for my walk:

1. I will try to go about 25 kilometers a day.
2. I will make no reservations for lodging. I will simply accept whatever accommodations are available when I reach a destination.
3. I will not be in a hurry (and will remind myself of this continually).
4. I will carry my pack the whole way. I will be forced to keep the contents light.
5. I will walk the entire way—no taking taxis or buses between towns.
6. I will make it a priority, since I am not in a hurry, to slow down and listen for the voice of God speaking around me or through those I meet. These are the "signs."

7. I will accept, within reason, whatever is offered me, as a gift from God.

SOME OF THESE became principles that I would carry with me long after I came home and would develop into what I call a "Camino for Life" attitude.

I MADE plane reservations for late March, with the intention of flying from Washington D.C. to Paris, then catching a train to St.-Jean-Pied-de-Port (or simply "St.-Jean"). I anxiously watched the weather in Spain—they were having one of the coldest and rainiest winters in memory—and developed doubts about my timing. I would not even be able to walk the fabled "Napoleon Route"[11] the first day, the highest and most scenic route over the Pyrenees, because it was still under a meter of snow. Leaving in early Spring meant that I would need more warm clothes than I had originally imagined, meaning extra weight to carry. I agonized over the contents of my pack, the choice of each piece of clothing. Would I be carrying enough? Would I be carrying too much? Would I be warm enough? Would I be too hot? As if to compound my anxiety, the French railway workers were threatening to strike...

In all my preparations, I overlooked my footwear. At one time I had hoped to walk the entire way in sandals, but realized this would be difficult in the early spring, with the reality of mud and the distinct possibility of snow. I thought that the well-worn-in hikers I had been using for several years would perhaps go the distance; this would turn out to be my only real mistake in all of my planning and over-planning.

I received one important piece of advice a few weeks before leaving, and it would turn out to be my first lesson of the Camino, though I didn't quite know it at the time. My friend David Landis, author of one of the Camino guide-books,[12] told me, "Russ, take less than what you might need. You can always get something along the way. The biggest problem is not that people don't have enough, it's that they have too much and they can't figure out what to get rid of." With that advice, I opted for less. And I would later come to be grateful for it. (And I later listened to stories from frustrated pilgrims who had to figure out what to purge from their packs.)

The greatly anticipated day of my departure arrived: Tuesday, March 27, 2018. I invited a few members of my small group from church and one of my pastors for a send-off.[13] We ate muffins, had coffee, prayed. With years of dreaming and months of preparation behind me, I received a blessing and we hugged and said our good-byes.

THE MELANCHOLY AT my departure diminished during the two-hour bus ride to the airport. Arriving at Dulles, I felt conspicuous walking through security dressed as a pilgrim, hiking pants and shoes, hat and backpack, watching the businessmen in their three-piece suits hurry through, impatiently checking their watches. I had a few hours before my flight, which I spent in a lounge eating food and reading magazines. My gate was next to the lounge and I checked the departure board nervously several times before queuing up for my flight, boarding pass ready. Showing my passport as I went through the checkpoint, I excitedly headed down the jet-way, conscious with every step that I was *on my pilgrimage*. Finding my seat, I stowed my pack in an overhead bin, sat down and began to relax. The rush of my departure, the sadness of saying good-bye, the anxiety about getting to the airport and taking off on time… it all slowly faded. I was on my way to live a great personal dream: walking the Camino. Everything I needed was inside a 16-pound pack in the overhead bin. My return ticket was six weeks away.

I was finally in no hurry.

The flight headed eastward, into the night. I ate supper, drank a glass of wine and watched movies, unable to sleep until the last hour.

Shortly before dawn, the flight landed in Paris.

I deplaned in a mental fog that matched the cold and rainy conditions on the ground. I went through passport control quickly and after retrieving a small bag—my hiking poles couldn't be carried on—I now had several hours to wait in the Charles de Gaulle airport for my train. The airport was not well-suited for napping and more than anything else I longed for a place to stretch out for some sleep. I was tempted to stretch out in the middle of the floor, but in my hiking clothes and with my pack, was afraid I might be mistaken for a homeless person. Mid-morning, I gave up on the idea and stopped in a shop for a baguette, coffee and a bottle of water. By now I was too alert to sleep, but too fatigued to concentrate on anything. I tried to read the French newspapers, but it would have been difficult even if I weren't so tired. I was relieved to gather this much: the planned strike of railway workers was still on, but not until the next week.

I looked at my watch and saw that it was time to board my train. Feeling very much the modern pilgrim, I shouldered my pack and took several escalators down to the *TGV* station that is inside the airport. I found my platform and

boarded the train for Bordeaux, wearily settling into a seat
facing forward, next to a window streaked with long rivulets
of rain.

The train ride to Bordeaux and then Bayonne took five
hours and the rain continued as I again attempted to nap,
body pressed against the side of the car. I dozed lightly as
the train whizzed at speeds of 160 kilometers an hour
through the French countryside. Occasionally rousing, I
could see flooded fields out the window; France was also
having one of its wettest winters. Giving up on sleep, I
pulled out my guidebook and looked at the maps of the first
several stages of my pilgrimage, beginning with the challenging climb the first day over the Pyrenees. My fatigued
brain began to doubt: would I be able to tackle it in just
one day?

In Bordeaux I had to change trains and I couldn't nap
on that one either. By then it was mid-afternoon in France,
but mid-morning back home and my circadian rhythm was
hopelessly confused. Surprisingly, I became more alert,
noting that the landscape flattened out as we approached
the coastal plains around Bayonne, my next-to-last stop
where I would catch the local train to St.-Jean.

Bayonne is an old French city in the Basque region, on
the river Adour, a few kilometers from the Bay of Biscay. I
caught my first sight there of dozens of other pilgrims. They
were obvious: packs on their backs, walking sticks tucked in,
hiking shoes on their feet. I no longer felt conspicuous. I
introduced myself to a few of them, some of whom I would
see again and again in the coming weeks: George (Jürg) from
Switzerland, Charlie (Carl) from Germany, Pauline from
France, Alan and Terry from Australia. The final train from
Bayonne to St.-Jean was cancelled and a bus would come for
us instead, meaning our arrival would be later than antici-

pated. I strolled the town for an hour, snapped pictures and bought a postcard and stamps. When the bus pulled up, I grabbed a front seat so that I could get a clear view of the countryside. Within minutes of pulling out, the flatland gave way to rolling hills, to small villages with their distinctive Basque architecture and their tightly manicured Sycamore trees, their limbs stretching out like the arms of broken umbrellas; it was early spring and they had yet to leaf out.

I was so mesmerized by the landscape that my fatigue was momentarily forgotten. The road wound around through small towns, passing farms with cattle and grazing sheep and barns with piles of manure. The higher we got in elevation, the more the houses reminded me of the Swiss Alps: long, low rooflines, with broad overhangs to shed the heavy winter snows of the Pyrenees. The daylight faded.

I got a lump in my throat again when shortly after dusk the bus arrived at our destination and the driver said, "C'est St.-Jean."

2

Following the Signs

Slow is the step of the going,
Of the riding, or the rowing
To the glens and bens that are strange,
Or the exile's isles of exchange
The horizons of unknowing.

Gaelic verse of the Western Highlands

I CLIMBED off the bus and in a great sense of wonder, slowly navigated my way along the narrow and darkening cobblestone streets into the center of the thousand-year-old town. This was the gateway to the Pyrenees, the way over the mountains into Spain, a way station for over a millennium. It was 7:45 and the street lamps were on.

Within five minutes I arrived at the Beilari, my albergue for the first night. There I was warmly greeted by Joseph, the owner and host, and after setting down my pack and removing my hiking shoes,[1] hungrily joined 17 other pilgrims around a table for a delicious communal meal: lentil soup, vegetarian lasagna, salad, cakes, wine, finished with steaming pots of herbal tea. My companions for the night were Europeans, Californians, Koreans and an Australian. We shared around the table our names, where we were from, a bit about why we were there and about how far we intended to walk the next day and even beyond. I enjoyed my companions and the conversation, but by 9:00, exhausted after a long day's travel, I carried my pack upstairs, unpacked a few things and brushed my teeth. I changed into my sleepwear, arranged my clothing for the next day and climbed inside my sleeping bag. I spoke briefly with my roommate, a young man from California, who told me he was "stoked" to begin walking the next day.

With my circadian rhythm thoroughly disrupted by jet-lag, my weary mind and body hardly knew how to sleep. I was excited and anxious for the next day and the beginning of my journey and drifted into a shallow, fitful slumber, my mind and dreams spinning with the events of the day, my hopes for the coming weeks, my imaginations of the trail ahead.

The next morning the lights were on early and by 6:30 my companions were seated at the long tables in the dining room, ready to eat and start the day. I sleepily got myself up and dressed, headed downstairs to join them, filling up with a breakfast of muesli, whole-wheat bread, coffee, juice and lots of fruit. Our hosts packed some of us lunches and I took mine back upstairs, where I put it in my pack. I searched my room for any stray belongings, carefully stowing everything away, then returned downstairs and sat down to write post-cards and have a second cup of coffee. Most of my fellow pilgrims were heading out the door already, strapping on their packs and adjusting their poles for the day's walk, heading towards Roncesvalles, 25 kilometers away, over the top of the Pyrenees, the first stop in Spain.

I lingered, not sure what to do. It was foggy outside and light rain was predicted for part of the morning. I had read contradictory opinions about how far to go the first day, some saying that given the jet lag, a pilgrim should stay an extra day in town to recover. Others said that perhaps a short day was in order; the village of Valcarlos was halfway to Roncesvalles and some of my companions told me that was their plan as they headed out the door. I was "practic-ing" not being in a hurry, but I also just didn't know what to do and envied the certainty that most of them had as they departed. I pulled out my guidebook and looked once again at the first day's climb over the Pyrenees.

A few minutes later Joseph, the man who ran the alber-gue, gave me the just the thing I needed. Standing in the kitchen, pouring me a *third* cup of coffee, he asked me how far I was going that day. I told him that I wasn't sure, perhaps halfway to Valcarlos, perhaps to Roncesvalles, but I felt conflicted by all the advice. With a calm certainty, he looked me squarely in the eye and said simply, "You can do it," meaning I could make it to Roncesvalles. I became aware instantly that this was one of the *signs*—a nudge from God—that I was wanting to be attentive to. So, it was decided: I was heading over the mountains.

Temporarily leaving my pack at the Beilari, I crossed the street to the Pilgrims' office, staffed by a French and German volunteer. I picked up a scallop shell to hang on my pack, a map, a list of albergues, and my compulsory *creden-cial*. As the French volunteer handed me the papers, she told me in French that I WAS NOT TO TAKE THE NAPOLEON ROUTE. She stretched open the map and, as if to emphasize, drew x's over that route.[2] "*Non, non, non!*" (Apparently just days before, two hikers from Scotland had gotten stuck in a three-foot snowstorm and had to be pulled out by helicopter.) My college French was a bit rusty, but I understood her well enough, especially the part about the €1,000 fine for rescue. Running her pen along the Valcarlos route, she drew more x's, insisting that I stick to side of the (busy) highway. She looked at me with a stern smile and with a "bon-voyage," wished me off, perhaps worried that I was going to ignore her advice and take the forbidden route, which of course, I didn't.

I wandered around town for another hour, taking pictures, nosing into shops, buying a pocket knife. Wrapping on my raincoat, I went back to the Beilari and picked up my things, then headed down the narrow street towards the gate leading out of town. I paused to take a selfie and record a brief video as I crossed the swollen River Nive. Looking down, I recorded my foot by a scallop shell embedded into the sidewalk. My pilgrimage was beginning. It was 9:30 on March 29 and I was a full two hours behind most of the other pilgrims.

SINCE MEDIEVAL TIMES the scallop shell has been the symbol of the pilgrimage to Santiago. Since pilgrims not only walked to Santiago, but then returned the way they had come, they typically got their scallop shell after *arriving* in Santiago. Modern pilgrims hang one on their pack at the start of their pilgrimage.

A *credencial* is the "passport" that all pilgrims carry, to signify that they are indeed a pilgrim, and is required to be able to lodge in an albergue. Albergues, hotels, restaurants and even churches stamp and date the credencial, used as proof at the end of the journey that the person has indeed walked the distance they claim. In 2018, the year I walked it,

327,378 pilgrims were issued *Compostelas,* or certificates of completion, in Santiago, the largest number in modern history. A pilgrim needs to complete at least the last 100 kilometers to receive a Compestela. About ten percent of those who receive Compostelas walk the entire 800 kilometers from St.-Jean.

SETTING out by myself along the road that first morning, sky grey, a cool, light rain falling, my mood darkened slightly. Rather than feeling hopeful and remembering the first sign I had been given, I rather began to wonder what on earth I was doing here, *not knowing anyone*— a husband, father of six children, grandfather of two, with another one on the way—setting out to walk an 800-kilometer pilgrimage across northern Spain at age 61. A seasoned and frequently solitary traveler, I felt unexpectedly lonely. Jane was eventually going to join me, but that was still over four weeks away. I knew only a bit of French, and not much Spanish. I had dreamed of this moment for two decades, but now that I was here I was having unanticipated doubts. It was Maundy Thursday, Holy Week. I was even missing celebrating Easter with the family at home. Was I doing the right thing?

The wet weather and my indecision about how far I could go that day had given me the late start. The Camino guide books and documentaries frequently depicted happy people walking with companions past ripening vineyards and rich fields of wheat, or through shady-green forests, chatting and laughing in an easy stride on dirt paths, as they take in the gorgeous scenery. Instead of being green, the trees were bare and there was snow in the mountains and for the first few kilometers I was walking alone on *asphalt*, in the rain. I saw only one other pilgrim in front or behind me and then just barely. *Four weeks* until I would see my wife.

As I meandered the hilly, quiet lanes, the rain slowed to a drizzle. My pace picked up, my feet and legs felt lively despite jet lag from the day before and the walking poles clicked in rhythm with my steps. I walked like this for an hour and began to turn my mind outward, taking in the scenery around me. While the leaves were not yet out on the trees, the pastures going up into the misty mountains above were a deep green and I noticed beds of begonias and other flowers, newly bloomed. Surrounding me were earthy scents of the damp world awakening after a long winter. I listened to the gushing streams, swollen with the melting snow, song birds and bleating newborn lambs. In spite of the dreary weather and my loneliness, I gradually felt an inner peace and decided that self-pity was not supposed to be part of this adventure. I was where I had wanted to be for so long, and I had all the time in the world. With that, a surprising phrase came to me— "It's a great day to be alive!" I didn't know where it came from, but that would stay with me over the next five weeks, even in the coldest, wettest weather or the longest, dullest stretches of road, especially when I was alone. Monotony, cold, heat, boredom, loneliness—they were all occasional parts of the journey; I was on my long-awaited pilgrimage, and they were to be appreciated.

Soon, small patches of blue sky broke open, the sun came out and with it the doubts and the loneliness evaporated like the mists on the mountains. The cool air now felt crisp and refreshing. I peeled off my raincoat, finding a place against a fence post where I could set down my walking poles and backpack while I stuffed the clothing in. All this walking was generating heat. *Maybe this is going to turn out alright after all,* I thought to myself. I finally spied pilgrims on the road ahead of me and eventually overtook a few more, saying *buen camino,* the customary pilgrim greeting, as I passed. The road gently climbed as I traced the French and Spanish border through small villages and shopping plazas, their signs greeting me in Spanish, French and Basque. I bought fruit in a supermarket, and after completing my first ten kilometers around noon stopped at a bench to enjoy my sack lunch at an overlook in Valcarlos. There was one more brief rain shower before I left town, so I ducked into a small warm café for a *café con leche* (two shots of espresso and hot milk) and a pastry while I waited it out. I set my poles against the wall, unshouldered my pack and introduced myself to another man entering, a German pilgrim named Ziggy. We sat and chatted about the walk so far that day; I was glad to be indoors and dry. The caffeine boosted both my energy and spirit.

When the rain passed, I bade Ziggy farewell and commenced my trek along the narrow and climbing high-way, squeezing tightly up against the guardrail as tour buses swished past. I was unnerved by the traffic and wondered how soon I could get off the main road.

The French woman in the Pilgrims' office *had* warned me quite emphatically to stick to the blacktop roads, the dirt roads being possibly too muddy or snowy, but the close brushes with the tour buses were too much for me. I came to a dirt turnoff leading into the tiny hamlet of Gañecoleta and hesitated, wondering if I should chance it. My map clearly showed that an alternative route went down there, but she had a big "x" over it. Moments after I decided against it, a woman in a small SUV came up the dirt road. Rolling down her window, she pointed back down the road and told me in Spanish that the dirt road was okay—I should take it. I was about to learn my second important lesson of the day about following the signs.

The road led downward into a narrow, rocky ravine and soon I passed the handful of houses that made up Gañeco-leta. Dramatic rock outcrops rose a few hundred feet on the left-hand side of the road; a stream was below, on the right. I knew the route would eventually have to go up again and within a few minutes I hit a steep concrete road that I supposed would take me eight kilometers atop the pass over the mountains. I felt surprisingly strong, striding confidently, my hiking poles clicking in rhythm with my steps, as I chugged upward. I was glad for the traction the solid road gave me.

I had gone about 50 meters when I heard a loud whistle behind and below me. I kept going. I heard it again, then twice more, before I turned and looked back and down. Was that whistle for me? Below, next to the last farmhouse, a man was waving his arms and beckoning me back down the hill. "What the…?" I whispered to myself.

I walked all the way back down the concrete road to the bottom of the hill, where I met the whistling farmer. He began to admonish me sharply in Spanish and while I couldn't get much of what he was saying, what little I *could* understand—along with his gestures—was clear. I had missed the path. He pointed to a wooden sign post and the yellow arrow pointing to the right, to a narrow path along-side the stream. He then grasped his own head with both hands and pulled it upward—I needed to keep my head up! Yes! I had been walking with my head down, deep in thought, lost in my own interior world, when I had cruised right past the signpost. I understood enough of his message now: on the Camino, you need to *keep your head up*. Don't look down, or you'll miss your way. Pay attention. Just to be sure, he gestured again, tugging his head upward two more times. When he was finished, I nodded in embarrassment and said, "Gracias!" Humiliated, I headed along in the direction of the arrows.

Now I knew there were two kinds of signs to follow on the Camino—the inward signs that we detect in our spirit, and the outward signs painted on posts, bollards, sidewalks, walls, rocks and even on guardrails. Both guide our way, both are easy to miss and both require our attention. I did my best to focus my attention on both from that point onward.

Arnéguy, along the French/Spanish border in the Pyrenees.

3

Can you Help Me Find My Girls?

My main purpose was to be where I was.

Peter Jenkins, *A Walk Across America*

THE UPWARD ASCENT from Gañecoleta was exhausting. I was now down to a single layer and still felt hot. Again, the route joined the highway, but then the route turned off once more onto dirt trails, this time climbing through a dense forest. As the afternoon wore on I occasionally sat on a rock wall or whatever dry spot I could find. I passed a young Spanish couple who appeared to be equally tired. The last stretch seemed interminable, along a muddy, slippery and even snowy dirt path. Several times I could see what I thought were the tops of the mountains above me as I ascended, but each time there was a break in the trees, I only glimpsed more upward climb.

There was a water fountain at one last junction of dirt trail and asphalt highway and I could see others choosing to walk along the road, which switch-backed upwards. I sat on a low stone wall to figure out which way I should go. I felt the fatigue in my legs, after seven hours of walking and climbing nearly 1,000 meters in elevation. I knew that if I paused too long, it would be all the more difficult to get up again. I sensed I was nearing the top, though I couldn't see it yet, and I pulled out my guidebook, which showed the top of the pass was just ahead along the dirt trail, maybe a kilometer away, a shorter distance than the road. I elected to follow the trail and in about ten minutes I landed abruptly at the windswept and snow-patched *Alto de Ibañeta*, the pass over the Pyrenees.

The wind was suddenly cold and biting, and I hastily dropped my pack to pull out my fleece, windbreaker and gloves. I turned around, leaned on my poles and savored the view: the sky was vivid blue and the late afternoon sun still bright, with occasional puffs of large white clouds standing in brilliant contrast to the brown and leafless trees of the valley below. To my right and left, the snowy Pyrenees were still clothed in winter. I momentarily forgot the fatigue in mind and body as I contemplated how many millions had viewed this same scene for centuries before me. I could hardly believe I had just walked and climbed over 24 kilometers. The town of St.-Jean, where I had begun, was far below, around many bends, long ago out of sight.

I was now in a busy visitor's lookout, where there was a chapel, a monument to Roland[1] and carloads of tourists. I crossed a parking lot to get to the monument—a vertical rock slab—where I wanted to have a photo taken. I met another middle-aged walker, a slim, short-haired and very friendly woman from Australia named Kate, who offered to take my picture. I posed next to the monument, feeling a joyful triumph.

She handed my iPhone back and then handed me her phone, to take a similar shot of her. As I gave it back to her she said, in a slightly anxious voice, "I'm trying to find my girls; they were just here a few minutes ago. Do you think you could help me?"

"Sure," I said. I started scouring the parking lot and grassy knolls around the saddle in the mountains. I saw groups of day hikers and tourists climbing in and out of their cars. I assumed I was looking for a couple of teenagers. I saw a young man and his girlfriend, maybe college age, but it was not them. No girls anywhere in sight. "Sorry," I said, "I don't seem to see them."

"They may have gotten a ride down to the albergue," Kate said. "One of them was not feeling well." Then it clicked—just as I had reached the top of the pass a few minutes earlier, I had been met by two older women, who both greeted me in Australian accents with a "well done!"

"Would your 'girls' by chance be in their *sixties*? I met a couple of women from Australia just as I arrived here. A man who seemed to know them got out of a minivan and offered them a ride down the mountain." "Yes, that's them!" she said. Mystery solved, the two of us decided to walk on together to our destination for the night, just a kilometer or two below the pass.

The path down the south side of the mountain was green and soft and as we chatted about the walk that day, the tower of the 800-year-old monastery of Roncesvalles suddenly appeared above the leafless trees like a mirage. Kate slowed to take photos, so I hurried alone along the last hundred meters of the trail, crossed a mountain stream and arrived at the entrance. The descent was easy and surprisingly fast. I turned to look back up at the snowy mountains and the blue sky and it sunk in: I'd finished the first and probably one of my hardest days—the climb over the Pyrenees, the natural border between Spain and France. I had gone over *those mountains.* I was on the Spanish side and now could call myself a pilgrim along the Camino de Santiago. It was nearly 5:00, and I'd been on the road for seven and a half hours.

I entered the monastery, a sprawling albergue hosting hundreds of pilgrims per night, where I was greeted by a friendly *hospitalero*[2] about my age who helped take the pack off my back, and then asked me to remove my shoes, which I did, placing them on a rack next to dozens of other pairs of footwear. I fumbled through my pack and slipped on my Birkenstocks. He asked me how far I had come that day and congratulated me on walking from St.-Jean. I paused to take in the airy interior and the smooth, ancient stone walls that had given refuge to so many millions over the centuries. I went to the front desk, got my credencial stamped and paid for my bed and evening meal. I paused for a few moments to look at the stamp, running my thumb slowly over it. It was beautiful, medieval-looking: a bishop' crozier alongside a *fleur de lis* inside an oval, the words in Latin. A wave like an electrical shock came over me—how long had I dreamed of this moment, crossing the Pyrenees and getting that stamp? For early pilgrims, this was the place where they first entered Spain, a significant landmark. I felt a part of that history, and I had crossed the mountains in a *single day.* Before I could contemplate this too long, however, an equally powerful wave of exhaustion swept over me, pulling me back to reality. The friendly hospitalero smiled, hoisted my pack on his shoulders and motioned for me to follow. I was grateful that he carried my pack up several flights of stairs, setting it down next to my bed in a dormitory room for sixty that would slowly fill to capacity during the evening. Recently renovated, it was bright and welcoming, fully modern, down to the electrical outlet for charging my cell phone. I was one of the first people in the room.

I thanked him for his help, paused just long enough to dig through my pack and lay out my sleeping bag and collapsed on my bed, propping up my sore feet. My legs and mind were fatigued, but I felt immensely satisfied with what I had just accomplished. I told myself that if I could do this, I can do *anything*. If I still carried any anxieties about the distances yet to walk, about my stamina, about the lonely weeks ahead, about my feet, I shed them like my pack.

I laid on my back for a while, nearly falling asleep, until I heard the clamor of more pilgrims arriving. I became concerned about having to wait in line for a shower. Reluctantly, I pulled myself up from the comfortable bed, rooted through my pack again and dug out my lightweight travel towel, soap and fresh clothing and headed to the bathroom. There I lingered under a hot shower that soothed my aching muscles. Afterward, I washed my clothes by hand, hung them out on a drying rack downstairs near the monastery entrance, and then slowly climbed back up to the dormitory. These chores taken care of, I laid back down, finally giving my feet a well-deserved rest. The room continued to fill up, and I talked at length to the pilgrim in the bunk next to me, an American from Minnesota, a bit older than me. He told me that he had started the Camino Frances the previous year, but had fallen his first day out and broken his shoulder, ending his pilgrimage on the very first day. He was back again, determined to make it to Santiago this time.

The room became noisier and more crowded. Considering how few people I had actually seen during the day, the crowds filling the beds surprised me. Yet in spite of all the activity around me, I closed my eyes and easily dozed off until supper.

RONCESVALLES–*RONCEVEAUX* in French, meaning
"valley of the berries"—sits in a secluded rural setting at
about 1,000 meters in elevation, smack in the middle of the
Kingdom of Navarre, which in the Middle Ages spanned
the border of modern-day France and Spain. Being just
below the Alto de Ibañeta, it was an important site even
before the Camino Frances, seeing the armies of the
Romans and later, Charlemagne, fight nearby. In the Middle
Ages and since, its bells rang for the sake of *peregrinos* who
might have found themselves lost in the fog of the mountains. (People still get lost and the bells still ring, though I
didn't hear them.) It has been a way-station for pilgrims for
800 years, its Medieval Gothic hospice[3] and monastery shel-
tering hundreds of thousands from France, Germany and
beyond. Besides overnight hosting, its religious orders held
Mass, served meals, cut hair and tended the sick. Even as
late as the 17th century, well after the decline of the pilgrim
route, it still took in 25,000 pilgrims annually. Now fully
remodeled, it can accommodate up to 183 per night. Other

buildings in the complex have been renovated into hotels and restaurants.

It also sits in Spanish Basque country, a region that has unique culture, food and language and which has been seeking to become autonomous and independent from Spain for decades.

In the film *The Way* (2010), Martin Sheen's character stays his first night on the Camino Frances in Roncesvalles, where he tries to sleep in an enormous old dormitory, a sea of bunkbeds. In 2011 it was renovated into its current, very modern condition. Many pilgrims choose to begin their Camino Frances here, opting not to walk their first day over the Pyrenees. This likely explained the crowds that first night.

AT 7:00 P.M., I threaded my way through the halls of the ancient monastery, passed through the courtyard with its historic church, then entered another building—now a hotel —where I found the restaurant. I took a seat at a table with other pilgrims—some new to me, but many of whom I had met the night before: Raymond from Australia and Sandro and Cynthia from Switzerland. I sat next to Janice, from Canada and across from two young Koreans, only one of which knew English. We were served a hearty pilgrim's supper of pasta, salad, chicken, and a sweet dessert, washed down with generous cups of wine. We lifted our cups in toasts to each other, celebrating the day's accomplishment.

To me, the dreary rain and the loneliness of the morning seemed long in the past, as did the uncertainty and anxiety of the evening before. We were all "seasoned" now, even if after just one day—a real "band of pilgrims." There was a lot of laughter as we exchanged tales of the challenging climb. I told about my incident in Gañacoleta, able to laugh about it finally. Looking at our full plates, someone joked that the Camino was "the only vacation where you could eat all you want and still come back weighing less." We compared notes about the weight of our packs, and two people across from me said they were already pondering which things they might have to ditch in the coming days. The Koreans—who didn't know each other until that day— talked (through their translator) of how they had found out about the Camino, how far they intended to walk the next day and in the following weeks, wondering if they would reach Santiago. Janice, who was older than I, seemed quiet, finally saying she had found the walk harder than she had imagined and was feeling anxiety about the distances. My own spirit was buoyant and I did not want the evening or the conversation to end, but after a few hours, fatigue overcame me and I dragged myself back to my bed. Passing through the courtyard again, I stuck my head briefly into the church, where they had just concluded a "pilgrim blessing,"[4] but I was unfortunately too tired to take in that part of the monastery's ancient history. Arriving back in the dormitory, I brushed my teeth and returned to my bed to arrange my gear for the next day. Slowly changing out of my clothes, I slipped once again inside my sleeping bag, inserted ear plugs and pulled a mask over my eyes, a ritual I would repeat nightly for the next five weeks.

By 9:30 I was sound asleep, unlike the night before, oblivious to the rustling and whispering of the other exhausted pilgrims around me.

PART II

Following my Shadow

4

Apparently, I Walk

CAMINO CONVERSATION:
Me: What is that you do?
Spanish Peregrino 1: I'm a policeman in Barcelona.
Spanish Peregrino 2: I'm a social worker.
Spanish Peregrino 1: What is it that you do?
Me: [long, thoughtful pause] I used to be…but now… well, apparently, I walk.

THE DORMITORY LIGHTS came on abruptly at 6:00 the morning after I arrived in Roncesvalles, just as they had gone off abruptly at 10:00 the evening before. I yawned, stretched my arms and legs, pulled off my eye mask, and removed my ear plugs.

An albergue can have as few as two to as many as 60 people in a single room (as in Roncesvalles.) Sleeping in a room with so many strangers was unusual that first night; besides public dressing and undressing and the general lack of privacy, the nighttime noises and lights for me were the hardest to get used to. Pilgrims snore creatively and it never lets up, though it is at its worst at the start of the night. I'm able to fall asleep quickly and that was a benefit in a room of perhaps dozens of loud snorers. Frequent and sporadic trips to the bathroom during the night meant light coming in from the hallway. I found I could shut out all the distractions with an eye mask and ear plugs.

A few pilgrims were already up ahead of me that morning, whispering to their companions, rustling their packs, dressing, stowing gear, collecting their poles, flashing the lights on their cellphone screens. A few had stayed up late, reading books with their headlamps, or looking at their phones (which can be distracting when you are trying to go to sleep); they were still soundly out. Roncesvalles had no bunkbeds, unlike many albergues.

I fumbled about in the dim light for my "nighttime" stuff sack and put in my earplugs and eye mask. I pulled off my tee-shirt and pajama pants and stuffed them in; then I removed my pillow case and put it in as well. Still inside my sleeping bag, I reached for another stuff sack that had my clothes and dressed artfully. That accomplished, I slid out of my sleeping bag and rolled it into its sack. My feet hit the floor softly. I was surprised that though they had ached so much the afternoon before, they felt good that morning. As I rose, I tried to be quiet, so as not to disturb anyone. I was to learn, however, that "albergue etiquette" was such that anyone who was not awake by 6:00—or whenever the lights came on—had no right to complain about noise. Gear stowed, I slipped on my sandals, pulled on my fleece, headed for the bathroom and then onwards to breakfast. In Roncesvalles this was in another building. As I stepped out into the early morning darkness, the mountain air felt damp and cold.

I found a place around a large round table with another ten or so other pilgrims and encountered my first Spanish breakfast: a long piece of toasted baguette, a cup of strong coffee and a glass of freshly squeezed orange juice. I ate and drank slowly, too tired even for any meaningful conversation with the others at my table, none of whom I knew. Twenty minutes later, fueled and caffeinated enough to at least get a start on the day, I headed back to the dormitory and after brushing my teeth, began my final ritual of packing.

I didn't carry a lot of gear, but even so, the contents of my pack seemingly "exploded" after my arrival the previous day and it had taken me some time the evening before to corral it all back into recognizable piles placed under the bed and on a small nearby shelf. These piles—books, electronics (iPhone earbuds, camera, charging cables) journals and pens, toiletries and medication, clothing—all had to be accounted for and packed into differently sized and colored stuff sacks. I went over a mental checklist, looked under and over the bed, down the cracks, anywhere that things could get lost, to be assured that I had it all. My phone and camera needed to be unplugged from their chargers and those cords stashed away themselves into a waterproof zip-lock bag. I looked once, then looked slowly again, taking as much time as possible to assure myself that I was not leaving something behind, especially my credencial, wallet, change purse or passport. Convinced I had everything, I loaded each stuff sack into my backpack, with anything I might need during the day on top or in a side pouch and headed downstairs into the large kitchen where I found a seat at a table. I wrote a postcard and a few pages of a letter to Jane, and made a few brief notes in my journal.

A large group of school children were milling about, talking loudly in Spanish, their adult leaders corralling them as they fixed breakfast. There were other groups as well; the albergue had been full the night before. This was surprising to me, since it was still the end of March, early spring. Who were these multitudes? Anxious thoughts rose inside of me: was I going to have to compete with crowds?

At the same moment, I calmed myself by saying, "I'm not in a hurry." I was going to be *deliberately* slow, take my time. *This was one of the principles of my Camino.* I took more time to finish writing and pulled out my guidebook, looking at the day's itinerary, or stage: 22 kilometers, to the village of Zubiri, alongside the Rio Arga, which I would continue to follow the day after into Pamplona. I pulled on my jacket, hat and gloves, grabbed my poles, swung the pack onto my back and headed out the door for my second day of walking.

I moved into the stream of walkers in the pre-dawn grey, met by a mixture of snow, light rain and fog. Several large groups passed me, chattering away in Spanish. It was now getting lighter and I stopped and had my photo taken at a well-known road sign—**Santiago de Compostela 790**. Walking a bit farther, I turned around to capture pictures of the monastery in the distance, dwarfed by its surroundings, framed by the light of dawn against the snow-topped mountains. Continuing on the road, I heard the soft *crunch* of my footsteps on gravel and thought about the 34 days that remained in my journey. Again I reminded myself: *The time and distance do not matter: I have all the time in the world.* My only agenda is to *walk*, to be *in the moment.*

The snow stopped, the fog lifted and a partly-blue sky emerged; I was thankful that this day was already starting better than the previous. I headed west toward the village of Burgette as the path headed into the leafless woods, through deep groves of beech trees with their long, sweeping limbs arcing gracefully downward. Known as the Sorginaritzaga Forest, or the "oakwood of witches," this was the meeting

place of witches' covens in the 16th century. I had to admit
the place still had an eerie feeling to it. I read a sign saying
that nine people had been burned at the stake during a
suppression of witchcraft, but shuddered to think of such a
brutal execution and the ignorance that fed it.

I continued on through open farmland, the snow-topped
Pyrenees just to my right, pilgrims dotting the roadway
before me, and arrived in Burgette sooner than I expected.
My guidebook mentioned a popular café, but I couldn't find
it. I took a few photos of village homes with their Basque
architecture—brightly colored doors and tile roofs with their
wide overhangs to protect from the snows. Giving up on the
café, I continued walking through muddy, open fields,
crossing small patches of snow, finally stopping at a café in
the village of Espinal for coffee and a "second breakfast."
An Italian couple was seated already. The café owner was in
the back getting their order, an egg omelet filled with potato
known as a Spanish *tortilla*, a specialty on the Camino. I
ordered one for myself, along with a slice of bread, several
pieces of fruit and a pastry. That would keep me going until
I reached my final destination around 1:00. While I waited
at the counter, a woman I recognized walked in. It was
Janice, who had sat next to me the evening in Roncesvalles.
Her spirit still seemed anxious and she eagerly joined me for
breakfast. While she had been quiet the night before, now
she recounted how she had sold her house and had taken to
traveling the world nine months out of the year. She was 70
and walking the Camino was something she had dreamed
of ever since she had seen the film *The Way*. She was a slow
walker and didn't know how far she would be able to go that
day or even how long it would take her to get to Santiago.
We talked for about a half an hour, but I had another three
hours of walking ahead of me and had the urge to get

going. When the conversation lulled, I politely said good-bye, gathered my gear and headed out.

FOR AS LONG AS I can remember, I have loved to walk. Childhoods of the 1950s and 60s were not filled with digital distractions, and television was not limitless. For my first 12 years, we lived in houses backing onto the woods. In the woods, and on the street, my imagination and feet ran wild. Our neighborhoods were full of children, so I was seldom alone, but even when I was, I learned to content myself in solitude, spinning stories in my head as I explored the outdoors on foot.

At age 11, I joined the Boy Scouts where my favorite activity was long hikes deep into the woods, discovering streams, ponds, beaver dams, mysterious stone walls and old wooden cabins. I loved the smell of the cinnamon ferns that lined the roadsides and the scents of the pines that grew in the old pastureland. I learned to read a topographical map and how to use a compass, even orienteering through unknown wilderness when I had the chance.

When I was 12, we left the edge of the woods and my family moved to Hinsdale, Illinois, part of the massive western suburbs of Chicago extending to the horizons of the flat Midwestern plain. The homes with their tidy lawns were arranged in neat blocks of closely-set houses on street after street after street. There were no woods; the only open space the manicured parks. My childhood seemed over—I felt imprisoned, domesticated; no more heading out the back door into the woods and freedom, no more secret fishing holes.

Before long, walking became my way of adapting to suburban life. I walked or rode my bicycle wherever I could: to school, to work, to the shops in town, taking all the time I needed, even after I got my drivers' license. I daydreamed about walking long distances, taking to the open road, unmoored and care-free, my identity nothing more than a walker, my home wherever I may lay my head that night.

In high school, walking became the best way for me to clarify my mind and to settle my inner life. In college, my love of walking grew and I sometimes walked up to six miles daily, to and from classes and into town. I enjoyed moving at what Arthur Paul Boers calls "the speed of life."[1] I read somewhere that walking conveys a sense that *we have time,* in other words, that we are *wealthy enough in time* to spend it walking. During walks my most creative thinking happened, and I began a habit of "mental writing," which shaped the thoughts I put on paper. In walks, I pondered my spiritual life, I prayed, I dreamed about the future. I thought deeply about what kind of life I wanted to live, and who I might want to live it with. I dreamed about becoming a writer. I dreamed about having a family. I dreamed of alternative ways of living; the counter-culture attracted me in those years (it was the 1970s) and I reflected critically on middle-class, American culture. I was determined to live a different way, a way that was simpler, less consumeristic, more natural, more down-to-earth.

I owned my first car shortly after college graduation. It was just before the "gas crisis" of 1979, when the price of gas tripled and motorists queued up at the few open stations, sometimes for hours. I was taking classes and working at the University of Maryland that summer, living two miles from campus. Out of necessity, with gas in short supply, I parked my car and took to my feet to get around. In earlier years, my walking had been counter-cultural, even spiritual, but now it was also practical. As I walked, I thought about how as an American I was part of a society consuming far more than our share of the world's resources, especially petroleum. This over-consumption drove an aggressive foreign policy and required an expensive military to defend that over-consumption of the world's resources. Later on, after the "crisis" ended, I continued to walk as much as possible, partly out of a personal protest of over-consumption and partly to continue to slow down and clarify my thoughts.

Over decades I collected books on walking, starting with Peter Jenkins' *A Walk Across America*. His 4,500-mile walk (which, including many stops, took six years) began with a personal crisis, a common theme in many books on long-distance walkers.[2] In 1973, the year he graduated from college, he went through a divorce and at the same time became disillusioned with the direction of the country, especially Watergate and the war in Vietnam. He wanted to leave the U.S. altogether, but a friend urged him to give it one more chance, so he set out to walk from one end of the country to the other. His experiences with the people he met transformed his thinking, his understanding of humanity, of America and of his entire life. I liked his idea of walking across the country; the freedom of an unscheduled, unhurried life appealed to me and reignited my earlier visions of "taking to the open road."

The idea stuck deeper that I might do a long-distance walk sometime in my own life, but before that could happen, I got married, started a career and family—important lifetime dreams and adventures all on their own. Still, the notion of a long walk remained tucked away over the decades as my life took shape, biding its time.

Twenty years ago, I discovered the abundance of public footpaths in England, a phenomenon quite unlike anything in America. There people walk ancient paths, even if it means crossing pastures and woods that are private property. Over the course of a half-dozen trips, I walked several of those, some thousands of years old, from Cornwall to the South Downs, to Hadrian's Wall and the Scottish Borders. They were beautiful hikes and they connected me with history—I was awed to think of the hundreds of thousands or even millions who had walked these paths before me. However, even there, one is never far from civilization and during my walks, I typically stopped in the afternoon for scones and tea to refresh myself. Such walking is more difficult in America, where fences and "no trespassing" signs dominate the countryside and heavily-trafficked two- and four-lane roads discourage pedestrians in urban areas. In America we don't have this kind of history and we don't have this tradition; the closest we come to it is hiking the wilderness and that requires hauling tents, sleeping bags and food if one goes for several days. You can't simply walk from town to town and expect to find lodging or a place for a meal.

A decade ago I came across the story of environmental activist John Francis, who refused to use motorized transport as a form of protest after observing a catastrophic oil spill along the Northern California coastline in 1969. He started walking as penance for his own participation in an economic system that damaged the environment. It reminded me of my own decision years before to stop driving in the middle of the gas crisis in 1979. His book, *Planetwalker: 17 years of silence, 22 years of walking*,[3]chronicled the inward and outward challenges of a life dedicated to walking. Tired of arguing with those who felt judged by his refusal to ride—and his walking—he further took a vow of silence that he kept up almost as long as his refusal to take motorized transport. In time he came to see his walking as a sort of pilgrimage and it carried him for decades across the U.S. and even to South America, while he studied at major universities and earned a PhD, *all without talking.*

As my children grew, my work life made several career pivots—a university administrator, a pastor, the finance director and CEO for a denominational publishing house—and as a necessity, we moved back and forth across the country. I still continued my love of walking and as a family we often went on long hikes together. These became some of our best memories. By the time my oldest children were teenagers, we had acquired two cars and drove tens of thousands of miles per year, even though I still felt an inner discomfort about it. Our familial resistance took on small forms: I insisted my children walk to school if there was no bus; I commuted to work by bicycle when possible. We currently walk to church—it takes ten minutes—politely turning down well-meaning neighbors who offer us rides.

Yet at my job over the last two decades, I spent most of my work days on my seat, behind a desk and in front of a computer screen, the child inside of me still gazing out the window, daydreaming of a life of walking, hoping I would not get too old to have my chance.

NOW, here I was, on the Camino, free for a month, my daylight hours *outdoors*, living life on my *feet*, at five kilometers an hour, in the fresh air, the breezes and sun touching my face, one foot in front of the other, paced by the comforting rhythm of my walking poles that powered me up hills and steadied me on steep stony descents or muddy tracks. Five to seven hours, 25 kilometers a day, through open field and woodland, crossing rivers on ancient bridges and Roman causeways. My dream from 40 years ago was being fulfilled: I was "on the road," unmoored and carefree, living entirely in the moment. My mind, my spirit and my imagination were unrestricted and childlike again and I felt extraordinarily alive. My life, my vocation, my identity for the next month: simply a walker, the rising sun behind me, following the shadow that points like an arrow down the road ahead.

5

Crowds

In my walks, I fain would return to my senses.

Henry David Thoreau, *Walking*

THE WALK to Zubiri took me up and over gentle hills and into stretches of deep forest. The dark woodland, with its dirt lanes (muddy in the spring) were bordered by bracken and low stone walls, covered in dense moss. The large beeches, bent into tortured shapes, gave the path a mysterious, fairytale-like wonder. The forest floor was matted with brown leaves, the undergrowth still hibernating. There had been crowds as I left Roncesvalles earlier that morning, and I saw them again in the villages, but by early afternoon I found myself walking long stretches alone. This is one of the most curious things about the Camino—a person can walk for hours, see few people, then suddenly encounter large crowds. Where do all those people come from? Where do they disappear to?

Nearing the end of that stretch, after cresting the Alto de Erro, the path descends a thousand feet into the valley of the *Rio Arga*. Just before that point it crosses a highway and I came upon a snack stand and a noisy, excited swarm of Spaniards. A group of road cyclists pedaled past and I found out later that the famous Colombian cyclist Nairo Quintana had gone by just moments before, hence the excitement. Since I was nearing my destination, and wanting to avoid the crowds, I decided not to stop. Soon the trail became difficult, alternating between large rocks and loose gravel and mud. My poles saved me there. The descent challenged my knees, since I had already walked over 15 kilometers. I had known from steep descents in the Alps that going *down* was usually harder than going *up*. In that entire last stretch I found myself alone again in the quiet woods. Having to focus attention on the road terrain can be mentally fatiguing, so I was grateful to arrive, after another two hours, at the swollen Rio Arga. The river is spanned by a famous 14th century Romanesque-style bridge, the Puente de la Rabia, ("bridge of rabies") that leads into the town of Zubiri, which itself means, "the town with the bridge," in Basque. Obviously, this old double-arched bridge was *very* important. I stopped to take pictures of its graceful stone arches from different angles; they sloped upward to the central pillar, its upstream side pointed to prevent debris from accumulating against it.

Zubiri is a small town, over 1,000 years old. Domenico Laffi, an Italian who walked the Camino in the 17th century, described crossing the bridge as "treacherous," with guards exacting tolls and threatening those who refused to pay. *My* crossing was peaceful; I only encountered Raymond, an experienced hiker from Australia, whom I had befriended my first evening in St.-Jean. He had arrived moments before me, and yet strangely, I had not seen him all day. We decided to look together for a place to stay.

The first couple of places we stopped were full, including a recommended albergue that was at the far end of town. I was surprised to see so many pilgrims, given that I had not encountered anyone the previous two hours as I crossed the hills. Returning to the middle of the town, we decided to take a bunk in the municipal albergue, an old school building, a very basic accommodation for, €5. It had a simple lounge/kitchen and mixed-gender bathroom in a separate building. We were shown a large room with about 30 beds, already full of pilgrims, and I didn't recognize anyone. I shed my shoes outside the door and placed them on a rack. I set my pack next to the bunk, and fully-clothed (there was no heat on yet), started to climb to the top bed. I winced the instant the soles of my feet hit the thin first rung of the ladder and I retreated to put on my sandals. I climbed the ladder again and plopped down on the mattress, propped up my aching feet, and in spite of the noise and commotion around me, soon fell fast asleep.

I was going to become used to that ache in my feet. It was a big accomplishment for me to walk an average of 25 kilometers (15 miles) per day, day after day, because I have flat feet. Thirty years ago, I developed an acute pain in my knees and an orthopedist (after telling me that "life is a slow downhill slide after age 30") said that it was due, in part, to my flat feet. Jane went to see a podiatrist shortly before my trip and she commented to him that I was planning a 500-mile walk. "What!?" he exclaimed, "he'll destroy his feet!" This worried her at the time, but I assured her that his concern was overblown—and I was right. On the Camino, my feet ached at the end of each day, but were never destroyed, and a night's sleep always rejuvenated them.

After my brief lie-down, I took a shower, changed into fresh clothes, and hand-laundered my dirty clothes at an outdoor sink. The temperature was cool and breezy, but the sun was out and I hung out my things on the crowded clothesline. I went into the lounge to write postcards, continue my letter to Jane and write in my journal. The albergue soon filled up and in spite of the cold, breezy weather, the front steps outside the dormitory were full of people talking to each other, or into their phones. People were going upstairs into the "overflow" areas. It was now early evening and Raymond I headed out to explore. It didn't take long since it was a small town, which worked out fine because our feet were sore and we couldn't go very far anyway. Trying to get ahead of the crowds, we went into to one of the local restaurants that offered a fixed price, "Pilgrim's Menu." It consisted of a soup or salad, a main dish of meat, rice or pasta and a dessert. A pitcher of wine accompanied it—all for another €8. As the previous night, it was delicious and I was ravenous after a day of walking outside.

Over supper the conversation turned to the crowds we were experiencing. I had not expected so many people, since it was still early spring. I had read that the Camino can get crowded during summer months, but this was still March. I felt some anxiety about finding a bed for the next night and I was tempted to start planning my pilgrimage to avoid the crowds. I even began to think of the other pilgrims as competitors. We debated about making a reservation, but decided against it. Raymond and I were going to walk to Pamplona together the next day and we planned to get an early start, well before the crowds. We headed back to our albergue and got ready for bed. There was a sizable group of Spanish pilgrims in their twenties. They were talking and laughing with each other with the overhead light on. I wondered if they would keep me awake, but minutes after I inserted my earplugs and pulled my mask over my eyes I was sound asleep. It was 9:00.

A little before 6:00 a.m., we got up quietly and packed our things. Inside the dorm it was dark and most of the younger pilgrims were still asleep, so we used the flashlights on our phones to scan our bunks. Assured we had everything, we headed outside. It was still dark and to my surprise, light snowflakes were falling. Our shoes were in a cold entryway, so I paused and reached into my pack for my warmest wool socks and exchanged them with the lighter-weight ones I had already put on. We headed down the street towards the Puente de la Rabia. It was 20 kilometers to Pamplona. Just before the bridge we saw the lights in an open café and went inside, where we ordered Spanish tortillas, toast, café con leche, and orange juice, which I proudly called *jugo*, (the word for it in Latin America) only to discover (to my embarrassment) that they call it *zumo* in Spain.

That was my first mistake of the day.

The second mistake—and this was really foolish—was thinking that we could navigate the wet, muddy and rocky trail along the river Arga in the dark. After crossing the bridge out of town and heading west along the side of the river, we realized that we could hardly see anything. Raymond had no light; we were hesitant to use our cell phones because of the precipitation; the snow was turning to light rain. My tiny keychain flashlight, meant for short trips to the bathroom or for rooting through backpack at night, proved useless for walking and it soon lost battery anyway. We tried to step carefully, but the trail was slick as well as rocky. To proceed would be dangerous.

Just then, we saw a light behind us. A godsend! A young woman wearing a headlamp was coming, her light fully illuminating the pathway. We asked her for help and she slowed her pace and walked alongside us for the next ten minutes as we picked our way over rocks and through puddles and slick mud, until there was enough sunlight to see well enough on our own.

The trail along the river, after we passed the ugly magnesium processing plant just west of town, turned out to be beautiful, once we could see it. Rain continued off and on all day long, with brief patches of full sun. This meant frequent stops to pull rainwear on or off. The Way alternated between paved surface and dirt (which meant mud). We stopped for a mid-morning coffee and pastries at a café in Larasoaña and several soggy hours later came upon the eastern suburbs of Pamplona, the city known both for Earnest Hemingway and the famous "running of the bulls" in July. We crossed two more medieval stone bridges before we arrived inside the walls of the old city, with its narrow and winding cobblestone streets. We were cold and wet and very muddy. It being the day before Easter, most of the city's albergues and hotels were fully booked. We tried several before we found beds with over a hundred others in the cavernous *Jesus y Maria*, the municipal albergue. Though it held a lot of people each night, the bunks were grouped in pairs, giving a greater sense of privacy.

I was glad for my zip-off pants; I took off the lower legs and washed them by hand to get the mud off, then hung them up to dry. After a shower and hand-laundering a few more items, we both laid down to take a nap, but not for long. The intermittent rain continued outside and the room quickly filled with other cold, wet and tired pilgrims. It was then that some musical instruments came out; a young man from Barcelona entertained us on his three-holed Basque flute and Raymond pulled out a tin whistle. More tired pilgrims came in and now, in contrast to the night before, I recognized most of them. We were a curious mixture of ages, about half under thirty and the other half over sixty. Small groups clustered around to hear the music and talk about where they were from and where they hoped to go the next day.

By late afternoon, too late to nap any longer and with the sky now clear, Raymond and I decided to walk the city with some of our other new friends, Paul and Lauri, from California. We stopped in several bars for wine and *tapas*, (*pinchos* in Basque), the tasty, traditional plates with portions of seafood vegetable or meat on pastries—appetizers, really — that are served before supper in the evening. The Easter crowds were everywhere and this was becoming more troubling to me. I had intentionally chosen to walk in the early spring, a time that I thought would be well before any crowds. What was going on? Was I going to have to start to get up early, race to the next town in order to get a bed? This seemed entirely contrary to one of my major reasons for walking the Camino.

Heading back to the albergue we heard a deafening sound coming from the Cathedral, the *carraca de Semana Santa*, or "Holy Week racket" made by a large *matraca*, a spinning wooden ratchet. Since the bells are silenced from Good Friday until Easter Morning, this was the call to worship and we followed the sound to the cathedral plaza where we stood in candlelight. The massive western doors opened and we poured in with the crowds. The Mass began with everyone standing, but soon fatigue got the better of me. Struggling to stay upright, I headed back to the albergue and my waiting bed. I was asleep again as soon as my head hit the pillow, well before the lights went out at eleven.

The albergue was awake and rustling already at 6:00 the next morning. My companion Raymond elected to stay in the city for another day, but with sunny, warmer weather forecast for the next week, I was itching to keep going, so I reluctantly fare-welled him, eager to climb that day over the Alto Perdon and onwards to Puenta La Reina. I headed down the narrow, twisting streets, following the scallop shells cemented into the sidewalks that marked the Camino. I was surprised to see a café open early on Easter, but gladly stopped to have a cup of coffee and pastries. The sun was coming up by then and the sky was clear—the first sunny start to my walk. Before long I was out of the city and heading onward in the fresh country air.

It turned out to be a glorious day walking in the sun and for the next two hours I approached and ascended the dramatic Alto de Perdon, a long ridge marked by over forty enormous, electric-generating windmills. My thoughts turned toward home and I felt a mild melancholy; this was Easter day, after all, and I would be missing my family as they gathered together to celebrate. Still, the scenery was stunning, and the air was warm and fresh. I passed the stone ruins of a medieval pilgrim hospital and water fountain as I climbed the last meters to the top of the wind-blown ridge, with its larger-than-life steel sculpture depicting medieval pilgrims struggling against the wind. The wonder of the moment soothed the homesick ache inside and I paused for photographs with some of my pilgrim companions. Looking westward, the vista was awe-inspiring: I could see my desti- nation for the day—Puenta la Reina—ten kilometers in the distance, with the village of Obanos just before it. I repeated to myself: "It's a great day to be alive…"

There on the top of the ridge a Spanish pilgrim explained to me the reasons for the crowds: they were on holiday! Holy week and the few days after are part of a long holiday for them, and many like to walk the Camino. The section from Roncesvalles to Pamplona is popular, with that city's Holy Week processions a particular draw. Many of the people in the city hadn't been pilgrims and he assured me that within two or three days the crowds along the Way would die down and I would find the Camino a solitary experience. I was relieved.

Equipped with this new knowledge, I might have started my descent, but instead noticed a ring of standing stones a few meters down the western slope, something easily over-looked by pilgrims in a hurry. I went to investigate and discovered it was a monument to Republican civilians murdered during the Spanish Civil War, in particular for 92 victims from villages nearby. I stared at the stones, about 20 of them, each containing a simple plaque, with the name of one of the surrounding towns where people had been killed. In the center of the ring was the tallest stone, with the words carved *No os olvidamos*, "We will not forget." At the bottom of the stone was carved a scene from the famous Picasso painting Guernica, depicting the massacre of innocent civil-ians during an aerial bombardment. Nearby I read an infor-mation sign. In part it said, *This is a tribute to the victims and their families who were killed for fighting for their ideals of social justice and democracy.* The Spanish Civil War (1936-39) took more than half a million lives; another 100,000 disap-peared, unaccounted for. This memorial is part of an effort to begin to account for those who had disappeared, many of them into unmarked, mass graves, in this case the victims of the dictator Franco. During the nearly 40 years that he ruled, their losses—quite substantial—were not allowed to be honored or even acknowledged. I paused in silence and contemplated this; not all of the most meaningful history of the Camino is from the Middle Ages. I would come across more monuments to the dead of the Civil War along the Way, a reminder of the ongoing struggle to find justice and reparation for the past and also of the current painful political divisions of this remarkable and beautiful country that I was coming to love.

I slowly picked my way down the treacherous, rocky western slope, finally landing on a level, dusty dirt path. From there the road meandered on the level through freshly planted fields of wheat, their thin green blades poking out of the red soil. This was a very different region than the foothills of the Pyrenees that I had been walking for the past three days—drier, and warmer, fewer trees, the vistas more open. I kept an even pace, passing through several small towns. A few hours later I came to Puenta La Reina, with its own historic bridge, and discovered, to my relief, that the crowds had already thinned. I easily found a lower bunk in a pleasant albergue that had a deck looking out over the Rio Arga and relaxed for the rest of the sunny afternoon.

I now had completed four days and felt like an experienced pilgrim.

6

Encountering the Magic

CAMINO CONVERSATION
Dane: You know, we lead the world in coffee consumption.
Swede: Us too!
Me: Aren't yours two of the happiest countries in the world? Maybe there's a correlation... (another reason to drink coffee).
Swede: I don't believe those surveys. I think they take them in July, the only month we're happy. The only reason I get out of bed in the winter is to drink coffee!

I WAS IN A FUNK: not enough sleep and not enough caffeine. I had left Puenta La Reina that morning just before sunup on my fifth day of walking, a full moon hanging in the sky directly ahead of me as I crossed the bridge out of town. Now it was mid-morning and I was passing through hilly country, with olive orchards, their leaves a dull green, and grape vineyards, their vines just starting to sprout. For half an hour, I'd been watching the beautiful and historic hill-top town of Cirauqui get closer, sure that when I got there I would find my badly needed and much beloved second cup of coffee. Maybe I would also get my second breakfast.

The sky overhead turned overcast and my mood matched it. Finally, when I reached the gates, I wound my way upward into the charming town, under pointed stone archways and through the old city walls, my expectations rising. But then for some inexplicable reason—I would unfortunately encounter this again and again in Spain—the village was more or less closed. Ten a.m.—nothing open; no café, just a tiny *tienda,* a shop with a few bananas and coffee machine.[1] Disappointed not to find a place serving "real" coffee, I continued to climb and arrived at the town square, where I was distracted by the fantastic architecture, especially the 13th-century church, Iglesias de San Roman, with its ornate *Mudéjar* portal. I lingered, taking photos, momentarily setting down my pack. This town was the Camino at its finest…but, no café. Taking one last look, I re-shouldered my pack and plodded out of town, walking on the actual *Roman Calzada,* the road with its bridges built by the Romans nearly 2,000 years ago. I stopped to take a photograph of my shoe on the smooth, ancient stone pavement and thought of them with a certain reverence: stones that were laid nearly 2,000 years ago were under my feet. I stowed my camera and looked at my guide book and noted that the next village was more than five kilometers away, at least an hour's walk. No second breakfast, no cup of coffee—at least not for another hour. Things were not going as I'd planned. I sighed and tightened the straps on my pack, hoisting it a bit higher on my back. Fortunately, it did not look like rain that day.

Twenty minutes later, cresting a hill, I was met by the unexpected: a funky sort of place, right on the path, pretty much in the middle of nowhere, with a "New Age" feel.

There was a gate on the path and next to it a bell with a pull-cord and sign that said, "Ring for Good Vibrations." I pulled the cord and the bell rang. I swung the gate and stepped through, following the road that ran below a low wall, an olive orchard above. My eyes were fixed ahead on a snack stand, something that I would encounter many more times along the Camino. A large sign said *La Volutad* or "free-will offering." Incense was burning and soft music was playing. The owner was busily laying out fruit and pastries and homemade souvenirs. But the first thing I saw was the thermos marked "coffee" and I headed straight for it.

Only pausing to pick up a banana, I poured myself a cup of hot coffee—it turned out to be wonderfully strong—and added milk. I climbed a few steps up to the olive grove and, finding a bench to sit on, pulled off my pack and gladly set down my poles. Lifting the cup and enjoying the double aromas of coffee and incense, I took in the scene around me. There were gently swaying scallop shells hanging from the olive trees, tinkling in the breeze; scattered around were potted plants, easy chairs, tables and wooden cabinets containing books, clothing, even walking gear—anything a pilgrim might need—all for free and all completely out in the open. I wasn't interested in picking anything up myself; the coffee and fruit were more than enough. I sipped the coffee slowly, breathed deeply and laughed at my good fortune, and over my previous frustration and bad mood. It was a wonderful moment and I savored it. A few other pilgrims appeared and stopped at the stand; some also sat down. The longer I stayed, the more my spirit and mind calmed and a sense of wonder returned. After 15 minutes, I got up and stopped once more at the snack table, this time dropping €5 into the donation box and picking out a neck-lace with an image of a scallop shell burned onto a wooden disk. It would be a gift for Jane. Hoisting my pack and grabbing my poles, I continued along the ancient road, feeling refortified. It wasn't just the caffeine that lifted my mood, but the utter unpredictability of it all.

I came up with the term "Camino Magic"[2] to describe these: the unexpected, the unplanned, the event that transpired just when my plans dissolved. It was the thing I found, but didn't even know that I needed or that it even existed. It was the person—or persons—that I had not seen in days or weeks, but who suddenly appeared in the entryway as I sat in a café. It was the open door that I came upon when I thought all were shut. It was someone I hadn't yet met, but who would become a friend. It was turning a bend and coming upon another pilgrim, sitting on a bench, who gave me a sandwich or a bite of chocolate when I was hungry, or who offered conversation when I was lonely. It was the hospitalero who would tell me just the right word of encouragement, or who laughed and insisted on carrying my pack to my bunk when I didn't think I could walk another step. It became the essence of the Camino. Before I set out on this journey I knew intuitively that this was the kind of thing I would be looking for, but didn't know what to call it. And now I had named it.

As a busy modern American, my life has been tightly scheduled, controlled and well-planned. I don't like having things go the way that I don't want them to. I don't like traffic jams, or red lights, or inconvenient signs on stores and restaurants that say "closed." I don't like picking the slow line at the check-out register. If I leave the house, I have a "to-do," or shopping list, errands carefully plotted. I check my watch often, leaving nothing to chance. I have weather apps, traffic apps, shopping apps, and map apps. I want to know where I am, where I'm going, how long it will take me to get there and anything I might encounter along the way. This is modern efficiency and control at its peak; it is very stressful and I don't like it.

Sitting on that bench and sipping my coffee, I began to learn to let go. I began to see that I could live fully in each moment, could surrender my tight plans, my stressful efficiency. It would take me some weeks, but gradually I learned to look for, to anticipate the "magic" that would unfold, if only I would open myself and be ready for it.

7

The Camino is a River

I am not a lone pilgrim out here; I am one part of a grand pilgrimage extending beyond the horizon and back into time.

Kevin Codd, *To the Field of Stars*

"I WALKED SOLO, with a few hundred—even thousands— of other people." This is what I say when asked if I went on pilgrimage by myself.

I would have preferred going with family, my wife in particular, but circumstances dictated that I go by myself. I went for solitude, but also to meet new people, especially the kind of people who take time out of their lives to do a pilgrimage. Solitude is a spiritual experience, but so is community. Combining the two is what makes the Camino a unique experience.

The Camino is a community on foot, moving at the rate of five kilometers an hour, a river of humanity that flows, ebbs, floods, trickles, meanders. Streams join it; it widens and narrows, but it always keeps flowing. It re-comprises itself daily; people leave, people join, people rest. This community includes pilgrims, hospitaleros, café owners, the people who live in the cities and towns along the Way, the people living ordinary, regular lives along an historic route that is anything but ordinary; the bicyclists who nearly hit you as they pass by, the slow strollers, the people limping from blisters, aching with each step, the fast walkers who will do 40 or 50 kilometers in a day; singles, couples, old, young, teenagers, retirees, people of every color, from every continent and speaking dozens of languages. All sharing a common road, part of a community walking with different motivations, but all walking together. I have never experienced a community quite like this.

The community of the Camino is a rich tapestry of people woven together by the threads of a mysterious and wonderful call, people from different life backgrounds, representing a wide range of ages and life experiences, and a wide breadth of humanity, both in the present and in history. I met other pilgrims from the moment I set foot in the train station at Bayonne, from my very first night in St.-Jean, and I continued to encounter new ones each day. Many of them became friends, some I presume will be life-long friends. Meeting people and learning their stories was one of the best parts of my pilgrimage. Aside from teenagers walking with their parents, the youngest I got to know was 20; the oldest was 74. Some were walking it for the first time; others were like Fred from Manchester, England, who was walking it for the fifth year in a row—and he began at age 67.

Since each person is walking it at their own pace, the community is never exactly the same. I was surprised at how people just kept popping up. I might meet a person on my first or second day, and then not encounter them for weeks, only to come across them as I ordered food in a café hundreds of kilometers farther on.

"WE WISH our husbands were going to walk with us for part of the way!" I had just met two women—I could tell by the identical haircuts and smiles radiating from their faces that they were sisters—Pam and Kathe, from Wisconsin. We were sitting down at a long table for a large communal evening meal in an albergue in the little village of Grañon. They were warm and outgoing, with a certain midwestern down-to-earth friendliness and ease that felt familiar. I told them where I was from, that I was walking by myself, but that my wife was going to join me near the end and walk the last week with me. They said they were jealous—their husbands were unable to come. They had started just a day before me, were walking it together and were looking for and appreciating the same experiences that I was. I liked them immediately and we connected repeatedly along the way to Santiago.

I had walked a little farther that day because I was aiming to stay in the *Hospital de Peregrinos San Juan Bautista*, in the village of Grañon, a *donativo* or "donation-only" albergue. Even though it was crowded that night, my guidebook alerted me that this place "was simple and much-loved for a peaceful, caring atmosphere." And they served an unforgettable meal, prepared by the pilgrims themselves, simple vegetarian fare eaten together around long tables that seated fifty or more people. It intentionally had no wi-fi. I was in the heart of La Rioja, an autonomous region of Spain, famous for its wines. As I walked, I passed a multitude of vineyards, their vines in spring pruned back to stubby thick stumps, flowing in long lines up the shallow slopes, as far as I could see.

The walk was long that day, 28 kilometers, and I was exhausted when I arrived. The place was rustic and old—medieval-feeling—attached to the side of a 14th -century church. I started up a narrow set of stairs, winding my way between the cool, thick stone walls, arriving at a spacious common room. There was a small fire burning in a fireplace in one corner. A group of early-arriving pilgrims were already seated around it in a semi-circle. Along the walls were bookcases filled with books and games. Two pilgrims from Korea were seated at one of the long tables, engrossed in a game of chess. A guitar hung from the wall. Looking up, I could see the ancient, rough wooden rafters.

I had already stayed a few nights in donativos and found them to be unique places, though the accommodations were not always the best and they were sometimes more crowded. Pilgrims chose them just because they were cheaper (you could stay there for free, if needed); for others, it was for the community. In the Middle Ages, the pilgrimage route had been serviced by places of hospitality like this, staffed by religious orders, freely giving their time and food to the pilgrims. Today the donativos are one way to relive that experience. Further, I enjoyed the hospitaleros, since they were volunteers and were *choosing* to serve there and who took time and care to attend to the pilgrims. They also knew what it meant to walk the Camino, since that is often a requirement to volunteer.

The hospitaleras at San Juan Bautista—two women in their late fifties from Holland, I believe—were the most gracious and welcoming of any that I met and they welcomed me warmly with a big hug. After a brief explanation of the simple house rules—including a request to remove my shoes and put them in a deep-set window along the stairs—they pointed to my sleeping space for the night—a large open loft above the common room where 20 or so two-inch-thick mats were laid out on the floor, no pillows. This was *indeed* rustic.

There were only two bathrooms for the fifty people there, so I had to shower quickly. I hurriedly washed and wrung out my socks and hung them on a line in the attic. Rummaging through my pack, I grabbed my journal, cell phone, camera and guidebooks. There was no wi-fi there and I headed to a nearby café where I could connect with my family and upload a few photos from the day. I had passed through Santo Domingo de Calzada earlier that day and was now in the region commonly called the "spiritual heart" of the Camino. My stay at the San Juan Bautista and its warm, communal feeling, was part of this rich heritage.

Many of the pilgrims had been enlisted to help with the supper: chopping vegetables, stirring the soup, setting the tables, filling baskets with bread, pouring the wine. Around 7:00 we gathered at the tables and took a seat. That's when I found myself with the Wisconsin sisters and also with an older American pilgrim named Peter, who was 74. He had been hiking and backpacking all his life and was used to "roughing it," as he said, so the two-inch mats on the floor would be no problem for him. He was on the Camino Frances for the third time.

The meal—vegetarian—was simple and delicious: lentil soup, bread, salad, wine and pasta. There were two large groups of younger people—one Spanish, one Italian—and different ones were challenged to demonstrate their skill at pouring streams of wine from the long, narrow spouts of the *porrón*[1] directly into their mouths. There was lots of laughter and raucous shouts of encouragement. At my end of the table the atmosphere was a bit quieter; the conversation was relaxed, alternating between abbreviated life stories, current motivations for walking the Camino and how many blisters we had. Afterward, everyone pitched in to clear the tables and wash the dishes. With so many helping this did not take long.

Then the hospitaleras invited anyone who wanted to follow them down the steps and through a hallway and a "hidden" door into the choir loft at the back of the church. Twenty-five of us found seats around the perimeter of the loft; candles were lit and the lights were lowered, except for the golden *retablo*[2] at the front of the church, which was illuminated. The rest of the church was in darkness, the walls emanating a deep mystery. We were welcomed and invited to sit in silence and breath in the atmosphere. After a short time of quiet, a candle inside a glass jar was passed slowly around and each person was given the opportunity in their own language to say a few words—where they were from and one thing for which they were thankful. Even with the barrier of language, we all seemed to understand one another.

In that holy space, the darkness of the church enveloping us, thoughts about sore feet or weary bodies faded. Just then, the pilgrimage had its own meaning beyond words—something beyond the kilometers that stretched ahead or the history that stretched backwards—and I didn't want that moment to end, even for sleep.

My mind centered and my body relaxed, I joined the others in reverent silence as we retreated back to our loft and prepared ourselves for bed. Without wi-fi, people were not looking at their cell phones (as happened at bedtime most evenings) and were simply present for each other. A young Catalan couple I had seen several times settled down next to me. The husband, Victor (pronounced Be-Thor), leaned over, and in a mixture of Spanish and English, introduced himself and his wife and asked my name. With a warm handshake he said, "Good night, Russ." I laid back on the two-inch mat on the floor and filled one of my stuff sacks with clothing for a pillow. The profound spiritual and communal experience that night was better than any sleep aids. In spite of the rustic conditions, I had my best night's sleep in Spain.

MOST PEOPLE ENJOY the Camino *especially* because of the community. With average lives so private and individualized, they find the common experience refreshing. On the Camino there is no status—it does not matter what you do in "real" life—and people can even choose to reinvent themselves. Masks are removed and pilgrims reveal their unvarnished selves. Day after day it is the same clothing, the same pack, the same sweat, the same dirt, the same matted hair (if you have it), the same snoring. There is no particular impression to make. Likewise, everyone appreciates simple things like a hot shower, a cold drink of water or a bunk bed at the end of a long day of walking. Rich, poor, athletic and fit (or not) it does not matter. Each is simply a pilgrim, like the many hundreds or thousands who are walking along The Way that day.

After my first week on the Camino, I had written in my journal, "Out here, trust overcomes fear." I learned to trust other pilgrims, to not worry who it is in the next bed. I looked around that loft in Grañon and realized that I knew the majority of the people there and I felt at home. On the road each day, I learned to freely share, to lend out blister tape or to give away cookies or sandwiches or pour the last glass of wine because I knew that more will be provided. Friends offered to share a load of laundry—and even return it folded! I experienced so many spontaneous acts of generosity—both giving and receiving—that it brought to mind the words of Jesus in the Gospel of Luke: "Give and it will be given to you, a good measure, pressed down, shaken together and running over, will be poured into your lap. For with the measure you use, it will be measured to you."[3] Who would not want to experience that day after day?

I didn't lack during the six weeks of my pilgrimage. I think I got a glimpse of heaven, walking the Camino—this is one reason why so many people who return to the routines of normal life have a hard time readjusting and why some feel compelled to come back and walk it year after year. My experience reminded me of the words of Dorothy Day, founder of the Catholic Worker in the U.S., a community dedicated to living with the homeless and hungry, who said, "… we know each other in the breaking of bread, and we are not alone anymore. Heaven is a banquet and life is a banquet, too, even with a crust, where there is companionship."[4]

That community, that companionship, is one reason why I will walk it again.

8

Feet, Shoes and Mud

Take long walks in stormy weather or through deep snows
in the fields and woods, if you would keep your spirits up.
Deal with brute nature. Be cold and hungry and weary.

Henry David Thoreau, *On the Duty of Civil
Disobedience*

MY HIKING SHOES finally gave out on the snowy final trek
into Burgos, my 12th day of walking.

Issues with my shoes had been building from the very
start. My first walking buddy, Raymond, had alerted me to a
problem as we trudged into Pamplona on the third day.
Walking behind me, he noticed that the outer heels of both
shoes were wearing off, meaning that my feet were tipping
outward with each step. I looked them over when we arrived
in the city and noted that not only were they worn to the
outside, parts of the sole were starting to peel off. These
shoes, not that old by my reckoning, were comfortable and
familiar trekking companions. We had done some great
hikes together, from the Swiss Alps to the Scottish Isles, from

the coast of Ireland, to the Appalachian Trail near my home, from coastal walks in Maine to coastal walks in California. Walking around Pamplona, I looked at shoes in some sporting goods stores and reluctantly began to think about replacing them. Passing through Santo Domingo a few days after that, I even stopped to try some on, but found nothing quite to my liking. I would look more when I arrived in Burgos, where I had planned a rest day.

Squishing through a lot of mud was my reality for the first two weeks of the Camino. A very wet, snowy and cold winter in Northern Spain, combined with thousands of pilgrim's feet, made for a messy, muddy churn along the dirt paths. The weather had turned cold and wet ever since leaving Grañon, with intermittent rain and fog. The climb over the Montes de Oca was the worst: nothing but mud, kilometer after kilometer. Nine hundred years ago, the area had been rife with bandits, terrifying medieval peregrinos until San Juan de Ortega[1] had cut this new, safer road through the thick stands of oak and pine in the 13th century. There were no bandits about as I crossed over; the only thing concerning me was slipping in the endless mud.

I passed through the town of Ages and stopped overnight in Atapuerca, a small village about 20 kilometers from Burgos. Atapuerca is famous—the earliest human remains on earth have been found in caves nearby—but I was tired the afternoon I arrived and it was Sunday. Even if the museum had been open I would not have wanted to walk to it that day. All afternoon there were occasional breaks in the weather, patches of blue sky alternating with brief rain showers, but the weather forecast for the next day was for continued precipitation—and cold. It might snow.

I registered at the new and very clean albergue *El Pere-grino*. I shared a room with some pilgrims that I met for the first time, including Fred, a seasoned Camino walker, aged 72, one of my Camino mentors. He was walking the Camino Frances for the *fifth* year in a row and he could walk far and fast. He had some principles, as I did, and one of them was that he never had a cup of coffee until he had walked at least five kilometers; another was that he always walked in shorts. He reasoned that bare legs dry more easily than a pair of pants. Even so, I wondered how he would fare the next day in the cold rain and snow.

Monday morning I began my pre-dawn walk into Burgos in a drizzly, dreary fog. The temperature hovered around freezing and the Way climbed upward into a broad ridge called the Matagrande Plain, part of the limestone Atapuerca Massif. The drizzle turned to rain and then to snow as I gained elevation; the dirt road wore down to rough rock, which with the precipitation, became slippery. The weather would hover between cold rain and snow for the next 36 hours.

It took a great deal of concentration to keep on the track, which meandered between white, fenced pastureland and woods. Fred, who had left an hour before me, told me later that he had gotten lost that morning, taking a side trail that abruptly ended in the thick forest. My guidebook had told me that there was an overlook where I could appreciate "great views of the city of Burgos" just ahead, but with the fog/snow mix there was no view of anything that day, nor was it even on my mind. All I could do was concentrate on keeping my footing on the wet, rocky path (my poles came in handy again) and keeping my eye on the trail, my focus solely on getting down the other side of the ridge safely and finding a place to warm up. I was thankful that before too long the trail descended and hit a blacktop road, the snow turning back to rain. My pants and shoes were now soaked.

I didn't appreciate it at the time, but with that descent I had arrived on the far-eastern edge of the Meseta, the broad Spanish Plain that I would be crossing for the next ten or more days.

After two more kilometers, or 25 minutes of walking, I came upon my first stop in the village of Cardenuela Riopico. I stepped into the first café, already crowded with other pilgrims trying to warm up and dry out. Glancing around as I shed my pack and propped my poles in a corner, I saw lots of familiar faces.

Eyeing an empty spot at a table, I peeled off my rain-coat, which was drenched on the outside from rain and on the inside from sweat. Next came my damp fleece. I squeezed my way alongside a long table, draping my layers over a vacant plastic chair. My spot secured, I headed back to the queue at the bar, ordered a café con leche, some orange juice, a slice of Spanish tortilla and a sugary pastry. I grabbed a banana off the counter and added it to my bill.

After paying, I turned back to the table and I realized that I was not going to dry off much, nor warm up much. With the door constantly swinging open from the stream of pilgrims entering and exiting, the floors and tables puddled from the wet and dripping crowd, it became apparent that the best I could hope for was a simple rest and some food. Warming up and drying out was going to have to wait for Burgos, still another nine kilometers away. Looking down at my shoes, I did not like what I saw: they were soaked, as were my feet. I had been pretty sure before I had left for the Camino that my shoes were not waterproof and now I was convinced of it. Fumbling through my pack, I found a pair of dry socks and gloves and pulled them on. I finished my food and even though my fleece and raincoat were still damp, I put them on as well, swung my pack onto my back, grabbed my poles and headed out into the gray damp air.

For the next three hours, I walked completely on auto-pilot: one foot in front of the other, not thinking of much more than my next landmark. I reached the airport on the outskirts of the city after an hour of walking, and by then the rain had turned into snow: quarter-sized, wet flakes coming down so thick they limited visibility beyond a few hundred meters. I had to admit that I was not enjoying myself. At this point, my pilgrimage was simple endurance; it was the first time on the Camino that I felt this way.

The airport in Burgos is where the Way forks; a slightly shorter option goes through industrial areas, while a scenic route runs along the river. I met up with other familiar pilgrims, Iago from Brazil and Donald from Dublin and together we chose the "scenic route" though with the heavy snow we really couldn't see anything. After another half hour we found ourselves in the suburbs and stopped for a hot café con leche. Briefly warming, but wanting to push on to our destination, we headed out through more mud, the River Arlanzon now on our right. By this point I was soaked inside (from the sweat) and out. The hood of my raincoat drooped over my eyes, keeping me from seeing anything more than the path directly ahead. Yet another chilled and wet 45 minutes squished by and we finally found pavement and the bridge into the center of the city, where my hotel awaited.

The night before, seeing snow forecast for the coming days, several of us around the dinner table decided to book hotel rooms in Burgos. Already planning a rest day, I jumped at it; and when I arrived shortly after noon at the Hotel Norte y Londres, I was even *more* glad. A friendly desk clerk, seeing my cold and wet condition, booked me early into a room on the second floor. I climbed the stairs and headed down the hallway to my room, my frozen hands fumbling to turn the key in the lock. I entered and within seconds dropped my pack and poles, peeled off my wet rain-coat and fleece, removed my other layers and sank into a steaming bath. I felt instant relief, drawing the heat into my frozen bones, and dozed off in the tub for an hour. Finally warmed, I emerged from the bath and put on dry clothes, washed out my muddy pants and draped the rest of my wet things over the radiator. I wrapped myself up in blankets and dropped onto the bed for a long nap.

THE LONG, hot bath and bed took me back fifty years— almost exactly to the day—to my first Boy Scout hike and campout in Simsbury, Connecticut. That snowy April I had spent a night in a heavy canvas tent, my sleeping bag and a plastic tarp the only thing between me and the frozen ground. I didn't sleep. Since it was so wet, we couldn't build a fire for breakfast the next morning and I remembered being thankful when we headed back to the cars and a warm home and a *long* hot bath.

When I awakened in mid-afternoon, I took stock of my gear. My old shoes would dry out, but they were pretty well shot. I decided that my mission for the rest of the afternoon was to buy a new pair of shoes, preferably waterproof. A pilgrim told me earlier that day about an enormous sporting goods store, Decathlon, a few kilometers from the center of town. I headed downstairs where the same helpful desk clerk showed me where to catch a free bus that could take me there. On the street I came across my friends from Califor-nia, Paul and Lauri and another friend, Patrick, from England, and the four of us headed out there together.[2] I tried on several pairs of hiking shoes, finally settling on a pair of waterproof Columbias. I also picked up a pair of rain pants, just in case.[3]

Returning to the center of town, the four of us met another friend, William, from Scotland and we headed out for supper and a farewell, since Patrick was heading home and William, Paul and Lauri were continuing the next morning. I would stay in touch with those three for the rest of our journey, though I never caught up to them.

I felt out of place sleeping alone in my hotel room that night, but I needed a restful night to be able to sleep as long as I wanted to. When I awoke, it felt uncharacteristic not to head out for another day walking, even though I appreciated the rest. I spent several hours in a warm, dry café, sipping espresso, eating pastries and fruit, writing postcards, letters and emails and updating my journal. I found the post office as I was walking the city, mailed the postcards and my letter to Jane (nearly two weeks in the writing) and bought more postage stamps. I toured the gorgeous and enormous cathedral, but was slightly overwhelmed by the number of golden chapels.

The snow continued until the afternoon, though strangely, it never stuck. I took more naps. I tested my new shoes and they felt good; best of all they were dry. In the evening I joined a group of pilgrims in a restaurant for some tapas. Itching to get going and a bit apprehensive of the long walk the next day, I went to bed early.

I KNEW that breaking in the new shoes would be tricky; I would alternate new and old shoes over the next three days, finally parting with my old *amigos* at the parochial albergue in Carrion de Los Condes. They had served me well, but when it came time to leave them, they looked forlorn on the shoe rack; I felt awkward abandoning them there, but I left them with a prayer that someone else might find them useful.

∽

PILGRIMS FIXATE OVER THEIR FEET, and rightly so. Walking 15 to 25 kilometers per day is hard on knees and hips but even harder on feet. Shoes and foot care are two of the most widely debated topics in online forums and with so many opinions, it is a source of endless confusion for would-be pilgrims. Should a person wear sandals or shoes? Or boots? What brand? High top, low top? Or maybe running shoes? Trainers?

The topic of prevention of and treatment for blisters is equally confusing. Should a person apply foot cream? Or Vaseline? How about powder? And what about socks? Wool socks? No socks? How about sock liners? How many pairs?

For each topic, there is no single, *right* answer, though there is simple solid advice: 1) Good preparation should include a fair amount of training, in good-fitting footwear that is broken-in, and 2) along the way, take good care of your feet, watching out for blisters. Otherwise, the type of shoe, the brand of socks, the application of foot cream— these are all subjective and it comes down to what works and feels right for each person. It also takes trial and error to figure it out.

Besides the forums, books about the Camino abound in horror stories about blisters, complete with grisly descriptions of bloody blisters on top of blisters (I saw some of those horrible blisters myself), of tears and excruciating pain, of walkers pausing or even giving up on their pilgrimage because their feet can't make it.

My first blister appeared innocently enough. Back on my fifth day I had stopped for a mid-morning break at a picnic place and removed my shoes and socks. I had felt an odd rubbing all day as I walked, and inspecting my right foot, there it was: a bubble emerging on my baby toe.

The appearance of a blister was a blow to my ego, small as it was. My first attempt at care turned out to be a mistake: I applied a band-aid. That only made matters worse; by afternoon the band-aid caused another blister on the toe next-door. Now I had *two* blisters. Brother blisters. What was I going to do?

The solution for my blisters, it turned out, was simple and the timing was sheer "Camino Magic." During that mid-afternoon break I was joined by my Camino friends, Paul and Lauri. They sat on a picnic bench across from me and removed their shoes to air their feet. I started talking about my blisters with the two of them and they offered some simple help that was the salvation of my feet: "runners" tape, the thin, pliable stuff that you can get in a drugstore. Laurie handed me a short length and I wrapped it carefully around my toes, which solved the problem. Lauri even gave me some more, in the fashion of simple pilgrim generosity, counseling me to apply it as prevention, anywhere that I felt a "hot spot", i.e., a blister in the making.

Knowing that I was maybe going to need a lot of this, I picked up a small roll of tape at a pharmacy in the next village. I now added another set of daily routines, for foot care. Each morning, after pulling on my clothes, I carefully wrapped my toes where I had blisters, or where I suspected blisters might appear. Then I set off for the day. At each break I took off my shoes and aired out my feet. After arriving at an albergue each afternoon and after taking a good warm shower, I peeled off the tape and let my feet air out, walking in sandals for the rest of the day. If at any time I felt a "hot spot," I applied tape.

With good, preventive care, I never lost an hour during the rest of my journey because of blisters.

PART III

The Meseta

9

We Pack our Fears

CAMINO CONVERSATION, OVER SUPPER:

Me: Sometimes when I take off my pack after carrying it for three hours straight, I feel like my whole body is floating away, like I've been pumped full of helium...

German: Me too! Unfortunately, the feeling goes away.

American: Some mornings, after a kilometer or so of walking I worry that the pack doesn't seem heavy enough and I start to wonder if I've left something behind.

Me: Same thing happens to me; I do a mental reenactment of my packing and sometimes I even stop to root through everything to see if it's all there. I call it "pack anxiety."

German: You know Scotty over there? His pack only weighs five kilos!

Me: Really??!! How does he do it?

German: He says he has the right "kit." You know, out here on the Camino it's like the opposite of society: Bragging rights go to the person who has the least.

I LEFT Burgos after my day of rest, eager to be walking again. I felt more alone than before, since so many of the people I had been walking with the first two weeks were now a day ahead of me. I would be encountering a new crowd.

The night before leaving I spontaneously bought a light-weight winter jacket, after my experience of being so cold and wet on the walk in to Burgos. I spotted it in a shop across the street from the hotel, but I agonized over the decision because I was unsure about the weather: would it still be cold, and might I need it? What if I got it and then never needed to wear it? I would have to carry it all the way to Santiago—it was a pound and half and moderately bulky. Would I be tempted to ditch it somewhere along the way? Was it a waste of money? Maybe I was overthinking it, just like my initial packing decisions at home.

The purchase was still on my mind as I left the city. My destination that day was the small town of Hontanas, a distance of 31 kilometers, (19 miles), my single longest day of the journey. The route out of Burgos is much more attractive than the route in—no industrial sites—and before long I was in the countryside. I stopped for a boost in the village of Tarjados: a café con leche and a chocolate crois-sant. I was breaking in my new shoes and I removed them along with my socks and let my feet air out. As in most cafés, a large-screen TV was suspended near the ceiling in one corner and I watched it as I ate, even though I couldn't understand the Spanish. Scenes of swollen rivers and flooding filled the news. The snow and rain had cleared away everywhere and the temperatures were warming.

I continued through Rabe de las Calzadas, which in the Middle Ages was known to be a treacherous swamp. And shortly after that, about three hours into my walk, I passed the small *Ermita de Nuestra Senora de Monasterios* or Hermitage of Our Lady of the Monasteries. In the Middle Ages, these were the homes of hermits who dedicated themselves to caring for pilgrims. I stopped briefly inside the candle-lit interior to absorb its quiet history and received a stamp from an elderly woman on my credencial. At this point I had been walking for over three hours and was beginning a steady climb. It was so warm that I didn't put on the jacket all morning; had I made the wrong decision?

All these doubts vanished as I completed my ascent and found myself suddenly hit by a stiff, cold wind; I had arrived at the Meseta, the broad, Spanish Plain, the high central plateau that makes up 40 percent of the country. The Camino Frances crosses it for over 230 kilometers, from Burgos, through Leon to Astorga, nearly one-third of the entire route. Off went my pack and on came the jacket. I zipped it up all the way and pulled on the hood. I never again regretted buying it—or the fact that I would have to carry it to Santiago.

IF THE FIRST obsession of pilgrims is their feet, the second obsession is their pack. This was true for me, too. One of my principles was that I would keep the contents of my pack light, since I was going to carry it the whole way.

Some of the earliest and best books on walking the Camino, such as Elyn Alva's *Following the Milky Way*, or Kevin Codd's *To the Field of Stars* chronicle theirs and others' tedious struggles with heavy packs and the injury and pain they suffered. Alva walked to Santiago in 1982, not prepared at all for the weight of her pack and the distance she would have to walk with it. Entire books have been written about what to carry on the Camino; I had two of these on my bookshelf at home, one of which is called, *To Walk Far, Carry Less*,[1] the title of which sums it all up. For a

modest investment, any modern pilgrim can outfit themselves with adequate amounts of lightweight gear, and
considering the abundance of guidance about what to carry
in books and online forums, there is no need to carry more
than necessary—ten percent of body weight. Even so, I was
repeatedly surprised to encounter people with overloaded
packs.

My own pack when full—minus water—weighed just
over seven kilos (16 pounds), just over ten percent of my
body weight.[2] Knowing the temptation to pack too much, I
deliberately chose a smaller pack—its volume was 38 liters
—an "ultralight," weighing just under a kilo empty. Two
weeks before I left I did a "dry-run" packing of my gear,
weighing each object down to the gram, recording it on a
spreadsheet as I stowed it inside my bag. I had thought I had
the bare minimum, but when I totaled it I was shocked: 10
kilos or 22 pounds. I put the pack on and thought about
what it would feel like after four or five hours of walking.
Clearly, I was going to have to trim down.

I pulled everything out and sorted it again. Gone went
the extra shirt and sweater, extra underclothes, my winter
cap, and my heavy rain jacket. I reluctantly swapped my
Chaco sandals for my Birkenstocks, saving half a kilo. I
sorted through and eliminated smaller items, such as spare
charging cables and batteries, handkerchiefs, and a writing
journal. Satisfied that I had reduced things as much as I
could, I deleted them from the spreadsheet and looked
afresh at the total: seven kilos (16 pounds.) I had reached my
target weight! And I knew that if I still needed something, I
could purchase it in Spain.

As little as I carried, I still had two items that surprised
other walkers: my digital camera[3], weighing three-quarters
of a pound, and a copy of *The Pilgrimage Road to Santiago: The*

Complete Cultural Handbook.[4] Over an inch thick, it was the heaviest thing in my pack, weighing just shy of one kilo.

As I trained and gradually increased my walking distance in the weeks leading up to my departure, I also found another thing happening: I was dropping the weight of my "engine," losing eight pounds of my bodyweight.[5] While in Spain, I lost another seven. My experience is that the weight of the pack has a far greater effect on the feet, knees and hips, than it does on the back. Many of the foot problems people develop are exacerbated by issues of weight. Considering that I walked approximately 1.25 million steps, I was glad my pack was as light as it was.

I had been inspired months before I left by an "ultra-light" backpacker, named Clint Bunting, aka "Lint" who is known to take as little as eight pounds on long-distance trips. He says, (to paraphrase him), "People pack their fears. Whatever they're scared of, is what they overpack for. If they're scared of being cold, they pack a lot of extra layers…If they're scared of bugs, they pack bug spray…If they're afraid of being hungry, they pack more food…" In essence, it's our fears that weigh us down, not just on the Camino, but in all of life. Free from fear, all of our loads, whether physical, emotional, mental or spiritual, lighten themselves. Along the Way, I learned that I could borrow from fellow pilgrims and that I could lend and give just as freely. So many of the fears we have in life are more in our mind than in reality.

The free sharing is part of the bond of community that the pilgrimage creates. I recall at least three times I found myself, mid-afternoon, taking a break and feeling very hungry. In each case, there weren't cafés or shops open in villages I had passed through, or maybe I'd just misjudged when and where I would be able to stop and buy something.

In each case, I came across pilgrim companions who were more than happy to share with me whatever it was they had. It was this act of receiving that struck me more than anything else: I find it harder to receive than to give, because being "needy" affects my ego. I reminded myself each time I was offered something, that this was a principle of my walk: I would accept, within reason, anything I was given. I also found this free give-and-take made it easy for me to share something I might consider precious (hard-to-find) and to not worry. This is a principle of life and something that I need a daily reminder about.

On the afternoon that I left Burgos, I met up with a middle-aged couple from England, he an engineer and she a Methodist minister on sabbatical. They mentioned off-handedly that they had already collectively shed seven pounds of gear, mailing it home at a cost of £45 (about $55.) It struck me that they had already paid for those items when they *acquired* them, and now they were having to pay to be *unburdened* of them. Other pilgrims talked about things they had jettisoned: extra shoes, sleeping bags, books, art sets, makeup kits, jackets and pants, a bottle of wine. They talked about the agony of deciding what to keep and what to get rid of. The hardest to deal with were sentimental objects, something they brought along to remind them of home: stuffed animals, musical instruments, and even a cheese-cutting board. These were irreplaceable and in most cases were reluctantly carried the rest of the way, though some chose to mail them to Santiago, to retrieve at the end of their journey. It reminded me of a passage in *Walden*: "I see young men, my townsmen, whose misfortune is to have inherited farms, houses, barns, cattle and farming tools for these are more easily acquired than got rid of."[6]

THE WORRIES and anxieties that accompanied my purchase of the jacket are a perfect metaphor for modern life: we want stuff, we feel we *need it*, but when it becomes a burden we agonize about how to get rid of it. Many of the things we buy end up in dumps, and not just the packaging.[7]

In the U.S. one of the best-selling books of recent years has been Marie Kondo's *The Life-Changing Magic of Tidying Up* (now even a Netflix series). Her methods help people get rid of much of their stuff, organizing and arranging the remainder so that it is easily accessible and recognizable. Million-dollar businesses and even entire industries have been spawned to help people sort, store and discard their excessive possessions. Another notable movement, "Minimalism" likewise encourages modern Americans to reduce the number of things that they own, in order to lead a more meaningful and simple life.[8] In evenings on the Camino as I laid down on my bed, all life's necessities were within an arm's reach. I spent very little time sorting, arranging and cleaning what I had. No need to de-clutter my life: keeping it all in order took just minutes. (Being an avid reader and wanting to stay off a screen as much as possible, the only thing I missed were my books.)

More than once I've learned—sometimes involuntarily —is how to live with few possessions. One summer, as I was on my way home from college, our family station wagon was broken into and practically everything I owned was stolen, including a stereo and records, a bicycle, guitar, and clothing. At first, I was devastated. I got over it when I decided to make it a spiritual lesson, recalling the words of Jesus from the Sermon on the Mount, "Do not lay up for yourselves treasures upon earth, where moth and rust destroy, and where thieves break in and steal. But lay up for yourselves treasures in heaven, where neither moth nor rust destroys and thieves do not break in and steal. For where your treasure is, your heart will be also." [9] I was just 20, but I decided that with the exception of the guitar, I was not going to replace any of it: things stolen once could be stolen again.

RETURNING HOME to a house full of things was one of the major challenges of returning from my pilgrimage. Having lived with so little, for so long, caused me once again to look differently at the things I own. I have embarked on a drastic de-cluttering; I see my entire life now in the context of pilgrimage: my journey through life as a walk. As I de-clutter and slim down and sort through belongings, I ask myself these questions:

- When was the last time I used this?
- Will I ever need it?
- Is this something I can do without?

Now if I want to buy something for myself, I put the item on a list, with the price. Most things sit on that list a long time. I think about the people I met in Spain who struggled with getting rid of things; I recall the ease of packing everything I owned in a 16-pound pack and heading off in the early morning, free of any great concern. I seek to live by the words of Thoreau: "… for my greatest skill has been to want but little."

10

Solitude

CAMINO CONVERSATION:
Me: Where are you from?
Soya: I'm from Holland.
Me: Why are you on the Camino?
Soya: I'm in a life transition and this seemed like the right thing to do.
[More light conversation follows, then there are several minutes of quiet.]
Soya: You know, I like you. You can walk with someone and not feel the need to talk.

SEVERAL PILGRIMS I met before Burgos told me they planned to skip the Meseta. They had heard it was long, dull and monotonous. They were going to take the bus to Leon, cutting out, at very least, seven days of walking.

I would not have skipped it for anything. The wide-open horizon, the long and lonely days, would allow me many hours of joyful solitude; the monotony would test my spirit.

The Meseta *can* be bleak, even boring, and the first day all I saw were endless fields of sprouting wheat, piles of white and speckled limestone, occasional clumps of trees (often clumped around the rock piles) and scattered pilgrims along the ruddy, dirt road. The terrain was flat in all directions, but the vast sky as wondrous as the ocean. The road headed off straight to a vanishing point on the horizon. It was still early spring, so the fields were more brown than green and it was all set against a dull sky. I only heard the wailing wind and the cries of the birds. The lack of scenery and sensory stimulation was a profound change from the previous weeks, where the Camino Frances traversed hilly and even mountainous country, full of vineyards, olive orchards, forests and charming towns and cities. In the summertime the Meseta is known to be treeless, with little shade, the sun intense, the heat merciless. In winter and spring pilgrims brace themselves against the strong, cold winds. Many of the small towns are just a single street, with few places to stop. Some villages are hidden in canyons, reminding me of Texas: you don't even know they are there in the flatlands ahead until you find yourself descending a steep cut in the road, when they suddenly emerge.

Eighty kilometers to the north, I could just make out the Cantabrian Mountains, a range that parallels the sea, linking the Pyrenees in the east to Galicia in the west. They were a constant as I crossed the Meseta. A few days past Leon some of them curve south and then I would cross them, but I still had nine days of walking this vast, flatland ahead of me.

∼

MOST DAYS ALONG THE CAMINO, I started out alone. This was intentional. At various times during the day, I walked and talked and socialized with pilgrims or hospitaleros—sometimes at length, maybe even for an entire evening. But the start of the day was almost always in solitude. I am an introvert and have always enjoyed solitude, even in the midst of crowds, and the Camino afforded me all the solitude I might want. In fact, walking the Camino was the longest unbroken time of solitude that I experienced in my life. I love the early morning; in a large city I enjoy getting up and sitting out on the street/sidewalk before it becomes filled with people and traffic. At home (I live on the edge of the countryside) I head out onto my deck first thing, spring through autumn, to enjoy the spectacular vista of the Allegheny Mountains to the west. In winter I start by a fire in the living room. I need at least an hour by myself to enjoy a cup of coffee and let my thoughts awake to the day. It is a time to read, pray, journal and reflect. This assures that my day gets a good start.

Some mistakenly think that being an introvert means I don't like being around people. It's not true—what it means is that as an introvert I gain energy from being alone. Now I had lots of alone: hour after hour of alone, week after week of alone, alone with my thoughts, alone with the quiet, alone with the scenery, alone with God. I thrived in it, I reveled in it, I bathed myself in it. It became one of the most significant aspects of my pilgrimage.

The previous decades raising my family had been fulfilling, but in recent years the long hours of stressful work had depleted me. Now, walking in solitude, I was replenishing my inner life. Writer and Benedictine Joan Chittister wrote,

> Solitude is chosen. It is the act of being alone in order to be with ourselves. We seek solitude for the sake of the soul. Even with easy access to other people we take time to be by ourselves, to close out the rest of the world, to

concentrate on the inside of us rather than wrestle with everything going on around us... solitude opens us to the wonders of the world without noise, a world without clutter, a world purged of the social whirl, at least for a while. At least long enough to immerse ourselves in the balm of simply being... In solitude we wait for all the noise to quiet in order to find out what we are really thinking about, what we are really saying to ourselves underneath all the layers of other people's messages that threatened to smother the words of our own heart.[1]

The Camino was foremost a spiritual experience for me. I am by nature a contemplative, and during the journey, my mind and spirit relaxed and my thoughts clarified. On the wide-open Meseta, with more time alone than ever, with my head bundled up inside my hood against the stiff wind, all the thoughts, memories, dreams and ideas, all that I had mentally bundled up over a lifetime—even any gripes and grievances—were loosened and revealed themselves. To my surprise, the negative stuff dispelled itself pretty quickly; in fact, it vaporized. I was so entranced by beauty, by simplicity, by the blowing of the wind across the wide-open sky, by the movement of the clouds, by the path in front of and behind me, by the wonder of what might happen next, or who I might meet next, by having all the time in the world, that any painful thoughts from the past seemed hardly worth the time to ponder. They were puny in comparison to the beautiful grandeur of my experience.

My own need for solitude goes beyond my needs as an introvert. Modern, Western lives are noisy and the noise of my youth—radio, TV, newspaper and magazines—has been superseded by 21st century digital devices and the Internet, which allow us instant 24/7 contact with the world, an unbounded stream of limitless data. My inner life cried out for solitude as an antidote to digital overload. Antxon González Gabarain described the solitude of the Camino this way:

> It's a place where there is no room for the usual bombardment of boredom, superficiality, consumerism and violence. A place where I can hold the silence in my hands, and hear the melodies of air, stone, earth and grass. A place where I can dwell for hours and days with that part of me that is neither body nor mind, gloating over the privilege of having all this quiet to myself, all the time in the world, and pushing. I push, and push and keep pushing. I throw off all the ballast, I purge the demons and charge myself with spiritual energy.[2]

As thoughts surfaced, I turned over the most fruitful ideas in my head, polished and preserved them. I felt a deep love and appreciation for the world well up inside, for life itself, for God who gives us all life, alongside a deep grief for injustice and ugliness, the over-consumption of the Creation. I felt connected to the past, to the present, to the world, to the ground I walked over, to my family and friends (even though I missed them), to my fellow pilgrims, but most of all to God.

As soon as I had an open stretch to walk, I took time to pray, beginning with my new personal reminder: "It's a great day to be alive." I had all the time I might ever need to pray, and it sustained and filled me. With hours of walking ahead, I engaged in a quiet, unhurried, listening attitude, contemplative prayer that was more of the heart than the head. I felt no hurry to get through it—I had all day.

· · ·

MY RELATIONSHIP with God is the foundation of my life. My faith, though an eclectic Christian mix, is anchored in my adopted pacifist-Mennonite community, with healthy influences of simplicity from the Quakers, Francis of Assisi, and Dorothy Day. An outdoors person and environmentalist, I deeply appreciate the down-to-earth spirituality of Celtic Christianity. Paradoxically, I love and am awed by the majesty and light of the great English Cathedrals. My social ethics—especially concerning justice, economics and pacifism—come directly from the words of Jesus in the Gospels, the Sermon on the Mount in particular. I was deeply formed by many years of communal life, where I became aware of my own selfishness and learned the freedom of living with few personal possessions. I have read widely and I have deep respect for those who come to similar spiritual "ends" through other means. For example, at 21 I first read the Transcendentalist Henry David Thoreau—a religiously disaffected, but deeply spiritual writer—and his book *Walden* left a life-long impact on me, particularly in my struggle to live in simplicity.

And now, adding to the mix, I was on a pilgrimage to Santiago, the most Catholic of practices (and I didn't even believe St. James was buried there!) in the most Catholic of places, Spain, walking with pilgrims who were mostly not there for religious reasons. But this pilgrimage was about the journey and not the destination.

At age 20 I had first read the Bible, devouring the Gospels in quick succession. I was willing to take Jesus literally, in particular his paradoxical statement that "he who gives up his life will find it." I decided to go to seminary, then into the ministry, but somewhere along that track we changed course and joined instead an intentional Christian community, where Jane and I quite literally gave up everything, including our personal possessions, inspired from reading about the early Christians in chapters two and four of the Book of Acts.[3] We first lived in a poor, urban neighborhood, then later in a rural area. There we lived a life free from concerns and anxiety about money. We stayed for 17 years and while it is now 20 years since we lived in community, its spirit formed me for life.

A decade ago I developed my own "daily office" to guide my prayer during the day.[4] My morning office begins with a prayer in the Celtic pattern, and I adapted it for my pilgrimage, knowing that I would be walking as I prayed:

> *I walk today by the power of God.*
> *I walk today in the love of the Father.*
> *I walk today in the might of the Savior.*
> *I walk today in the renewing of the Spirit.*

> *I walk today to the freshness of the earth*
> *To the brightness of the sun,*
> *To the glory of the light*
> *To the life-giving rain:*
> *I walk today.*

> *To the journey of life, I walk today.*
> *To renewal and freshness, I walk today.*
> *To new encounters and challenges, I walk today.*
> *To those I meet and might help, I walk today.*

> *I walk today by the power of God.*
> *I walk today in the Love of the Father.*
> *I walk today in the might of the Savior*
> *I walk today in the renewing of the Spirit*

Each day along the Camino, in the peaceful quiet, I thanked God for my family, naming each person, and praying for them. I prayed for old friends, for fellow pilgrims. I thanked God for my pilgrimage, for new friends I was meeting. I prayed for safety and for health. I prayed that I might be alert to the needs of others. Prayer is not just a one-way street—it involves just as much listening as anything. What I received most from God in that time was inner quietness and contentment, a deeper awareness of the world around and far beyond me. The silence soaked into me, giving to me its own meaning, beyond words.

In quiet contemplation—in solitude—I found God to be my walking companion, someone who could walk alongside me and not feel the need to talk.

With an early bedtime—I was in bed most nights by 9:30—I was often awake in the middle of the night for as much as an hour. This is the time the ancients called the night "watches,"[5] as in Psalm 63 where the psalmist says, "I mused on you in the watches of the night." I consoled myself through prayer, bringing to mind a passage from Psalm 143, "let the dawn bring news of your faithful love."

Walking in solitude also clarified my mind—new thoughts and old dreams emerged—and that's where I found God speaking to me the most. Dots connected. I felt like some pattern inside was being repaired, and I didn't even know it was broken. As Chittister says, "It is here in the well of the self that our unfinished self, our real self, lies waiting for attention."[6]

As my mind became clearer, I started writing; at first it was just letters and postcards, but it expanded into written postings on social media for friends.[7] It was as if there was an abundance of creativity waiting for its opportunity to surface. The threads of wonder that I discovered along the ancient road—whether a wonder of nature, or of the culture or of history—were woven into a rich tapestry. Each day was, "a great day to be alive." Life became richer and I felt an irresistible urge to express this through my lifelong dream to write.

If I wanted to share my thoughts in the present, I had to write them on a smartphone, which was limiting: it took longer. But it did not matter; I had all the time in the world and I was not in a hurry.

LONELINESS CAME WITH THE SOLITUDE. I missed my wife and children and my friends at home. This contained a paradox; being alone, my life became richer. The richer it became, the more I wanted to share it with those I loved the dearest, and yet they weren't with me. I took pictures and sent home messages and enjoyed their responses. As much as I loved the solitude, I resolved that if I walked the whole thing again, I would do at least part of it with a member of my family.

I overcame the challenge of loneliness by reaching out to others and making friends. This began my very first day and was not hard. I can be somewhat reserved around people I don't know, but when you are on the Camino, you know automatically you have something in common with other pilgrims. (Who else has all the time and the motivation to walk 500 miles?) For the month I walked the Camino by myself, I was seldom alone at the end of the day. I purposely stayed each night in albergues with, on average, a few dozen others, but sometimes with hundreds of others. I enjoyed conversations at supper—communal meals being a highlight of each day—and there were often pilgrim masses or blessing services in the evenings. There was a certain comfort and camaraderie at night as I went to sleep, lying down in a room of random people who were all on a pilgrimage and now had become my friends.

My days of loneliness had a consolation; I could look forward to the fact that Jane would be joining me by the end of the month and that I could share with her my new wealth of experiences. I might have an ultimate destination, which was Santiago, but the time alone gave me a second destination: Sarria, April 27, the day Jane was going to join me. As I crossed the Meseta, I counted down the days ahead, still reveling in the solitude. I was enjoying every step of the way until that day came.

Camino
de Santiago →

Calzada de
Piedra →

A SANTIAGO 401 →
www.cafeterialoscondes.com

11

I'm not in a hurry

Out here I blast myself free from the official and unofficial versions of myself. I open the door to the genuine sensitivity and morality that lives inside me. I unveil my clean, honest face that the world says I must keep covered and censored… Yes sir, out here I abandon the boredom, superficiality, consumerism and violence that explode continuously from the television, radio, shopping center, the mayor, the priest and the pharmacist; the mortgage, the aseptic life of the internet and "wireless communication" that follows me into the very toilet.

Antxon Gonzáles Gabarain, aka "Bolitx", *The Great Westward Walk*

I HAD the "I'm not in a hurry" thing down pretty well by my third week, but not without effort. The first few mornings of my pilgrimage the quiet rustling of my neighbors around 6:00 was my signal to wake up and get going. I felt a strange internal pressure to hurry, as if we were all in a competition or a race. I don't know where it came from, or why I thought it, but there it was; it was not rational.

That's when I said to myself, "I'm not in a hurry," and began to relax. The statement became my mantra. I said it not only first thing in the morning, I said it to myself as I sat in cafés mid-morning, savoring a café con leche; I said it to myself as I walked long stretches of the road and younger, faster groups of pilgrims bore down on me from behind. I had to say it to myself if I sat on the side of the trail for 15 minutes, just to rest my feet. *Don't be silly—this is not a race*, I thought to myself, again and again. Yet the urge to hurry, the belief that time is a scarce commodity, is *very* deeply rooted.

The principle, "I will not be in a hurry," was not just a goal for this pilgrimage, it was a new life discipline to learn. It came to me eventually that what I was doing was "cultivating slowness" taking a more deliberate and thoughtful approach to each moment of life. But learning a new habit was not going to be easy; it had taken me a lifetime to develop the old one. To change was going to require a conspicuous effort:

I cultivated slowness by intentionally taking extra time to do things that I normally might rush through, like putting things in my pack, or eating my first (or second!) breakfast.

I cultivated slowness by taking time for photography. I took pictures of doors, windows, signs, houses, churches, fields of grain and vineyards. I changed angles, looking for the best shot.

I cultivated slowness by seeing each pilgrim as a brother or sister when I came alongside them on the path, greeting them with *"Buen camino, hermano,"* and striking up conversations, even though it meant slowing my pace.

I cultivated slowness when waiting in line in a shop, or a café, or in my albergue at the end of the day and allowing others to go in front of me.

"I'm not in a hurry," I reminded myself.

I FIRST BECAME aware that I suffered from something called "hurry sickness" about 15 years ago. I was a pastor and struggled spiritually with the pace of modern life, both personally and in the lives of others. I came across its definition in a book, "… a continuous struggle and unremitting attempt to accomplish or achieve more and more things or participate in more and more events in less and less time, frequently in the face of opposition, real or imagined, from other persons."[1] The author said we need to "ruthlessly eliminate" hurry from our lives as a requirement of spiritual health and that resonated with me. Some of the symptoms he mentioned:

- Constantly speeding up daily activities; a haunting fear that there are just not enough hours in the day to do what needs to be done.
- Reading faster, talking faster, and, when listening, nodding faster to encourage the talker to accelerate.
- Inwardly chafing whenever I have to wait (as in a line in the store).
- Multi-tasking.
- Accumulating clutter. For example, acquiring stacks of books and magazines and then feeling guilty for not reading them. Or buying time-

saving gadgets and not taking the time to read the instructions on how to use them.

- Feeling weighed down by the burden of all the things I have failed to say no to.
- Superficiality—trading wisdom for information; exchanging depth for breadth. I felt at times that my life was a "mile-wide and an inch deep," to quote a friend.
- Sunset fatigue. Those who need our love the most, those to whom we are most committed, end up getting the leftovers of our time and energy. Sunset fatigue is being too tired, or too drained, or too preoccupied, to love the people to whom we have made the deepest promises.
- A loss of gratitude and wonder.
- Indulging in self-destructive escapes from fatigue, e.g., computer games, or mindlessly looking at TV.

This list of symptoms is from over a decade ago, before the invention of the smartphone, which has made our lives faster-paced, busier and even more distracted, and before most older adults had discovered social media. It is one of the ironies of American life that busyness is a status symbol; the busier we are, the more important we must be.

Even as I read and thought about "hurry sickness"—and vowed to slow down—my life, between work and home, ironically became busier. In one three-year period, we relocated our family twice, moves necessitated by work. I barely had time to settle in to one place before I had to move to another. The moves and changes in work took a toll, even as I excelled at my job, received promotions and maintained an active role as a husband and father. I reached the "pinnacle" of my career, becoming publisher for the Mennonite Churches in North America, a role which required much travel.

In the same years both of my parents and my brother-in-law died. Besides dealing with the grief—which was hard, as busy as I was—I reflected often about how soon our lives can end and how important it is to live as fully as we can, while we can. I re-read Thoreau's *Walden* then and was struck when I came across this passage in his chapter on "Sounds":

> I love a broad margin to my life. Sometimes in a summer morning, having taken my accustomed bath, I sat in my sunny doorway from sunrise till noon, rapt in a revery, amidst the pines and hickories and sumachs, in undis-turbed solitude and stillness, while the birds sang around me or flitted noiseless through the house, until by the sun falling in at my west window, or the noise of some travel-er's wagon on the distant highway, I was reminded of the lapse of time. I grew in those seasons like corn in the night and they were far better than any work of the hands would have been. They were not time subtracted from my life, but so much over and above my usual allowance... The day advanced as if to light some work of mine; it was morning, and lo, now it is evening, and nothing memo-rable is accomplished. Instead of singing like the birds, I silently smiled at my good fortune... this was sheer idle-ness to my fellow-townsmen no doubt; but if the birds and flowers had tried me by their standard, I should have not been found wanting.[2]

Imagine having the time to simply sit on the front step and listen to the birds. More than anything, I wanted the freedom to do that; I *needed* the freedom to do that. I wanted to change, to slow down my life, to have more margin and more time, but struggled with the how and when. Then, after turning 60 and deciding to leave my work and take a year's sabbatical, I laid plans to walk the Camino.

Walking across the Meseta, now I had that broad margin, and the time I'd craved. I savored every moment. I was not in a hurry.

On my 15th day of walking, I felt that change happening. Around mid-morning I was trekking across a particularly featureless part of the Camino: a flat, straight gravel path that ran alongside the highway for at least five kilometers. The day had started out with light rain and the sky was gray. It was April 13th, the anniversary of my mother's death in 2007. She had died rather unpredictably from colon cancer —just six months from diagnosis to death. I was reflecting on her life and her sudden passing as I overtook another pilgrim, Frank.

I'd seen Frank quite a few times ever since I'd left Pamplona, on my fourth day of walking. He was around 50 years old, and had a large pack with a distinctive orange cover. We'd stayed in the same albergues various times over the previous two weeks—we both liked the donativos. I discovered that he was from Germany and he enjoyed the fact that I knew a bit of German, smiling when I greeted him in the morning with *"Hast du gut geschlafen?"* Others told me he had walked a long way already; he was from Frank-furt and had set out on foot from there. By the time he had reached St.-Jean at the base of the Pyrenees, the starting place for most of us, he had *already* covered 1,000 kilometers.

We were both on our way to Carrion de los Condes and were about a kilometer from the tiny village of Población de Campos. I was walking faster than he was. Typically, I would walk alongside and say, *"Buen camino, hermano,"* and continue on my way.

But that day I felt an urge to linger with him—one of those inner "signs" I was trying to pay attention to—and after my greeting, struck up a conversation. He told me had left his home about three months earlier to walk all the way to Santiago. His pack was so large because he was carrying a tent and winter clothing. *This is a genuine pilgrim*, I thought to myself. I asked him why he was walking the Camino. What he said next surprised me.

Three years earlier he had been diagnosed with colon cancer and had gone through chemo. "It was awful, but I went into remission." He had tried to walk part of the Camino right after it but felt sick and after a week he'd quit. Then just the previous December the cancer came back and the doctor told him he had maybe only a year to live. "He said I should try chemo again, to prolong my life," but he remembered how much he hated it and refused. Instead, he decided to try to walk to Santiago de Compostela again, and ask God what he should do. Just then he pulled out his driver's license and showed me his photo, pointing out how much rounder his face had been a few years earlier, when it was taken. "I've lost 40 kilos."

I was silent for a moment, taking in what he had just said to me. After a brief silence, I told him about my mother and how she had died eleven years ago that very day. I told him about how I'd been with her when she'd been under-going chemo and that because of her I knew how awful both the cancer and the treatment were. We talked more and he told me about his hopes and fears for the future; he told me about his daughter, a nurse, back in Germany. He missed her.

I thought to myself, *this encounter is not a coincidence.*

We walked together in silence for a bit longer and then he asked me if he could borrow a euro for a cup of coffee. This was not a difficult request, but I replied, "How about if I buy you a cup in the next village?" Within minutes, we came into Población and stopped in a café, where I bought him a café con Leche. As we drank it, he explained that he was on a monthly disability allowance and that his money would not come through for two more days; could I lend him a few euros more? He hadn't eaten yet that day and I realized then that he must be penniless. I also understood why he tried to stay at the donativos. "No problem," I said as I handed him €20. I paused before I put away my wallet, then handed him €20 more, saying, "I decided a week ago that I would always accept whatever I was given on the Camino, and I've been given to generously. I also wish to give likewise. I don't need to have this back." He thanked me, insisting he would repay. After a while the conversation slowed down. I knew he felt a bit self-conscious—maybe even embarrassed—so I got up, grabbed my pack and poles, saying, *"Buen camino, hermano."*

I saw him repeatedly over the next days, until we reached Leon, where I finally lost track of him. He continued to thank me for the cash, and though he said he would repay me, I was secretly glad he didn't. Having been able to share freely with him felt like a privilege—worth far more than the cost.

This experience was one of the most important I had on my pilgrimage. I heard the inner-prompting to stop and talk with Frank only because I had *deliberately slowed down enough* to hear the "inner signs" that are as important on the Camino as the physical signs.

As a daily reminder of this I now have a note stuck to the door of my refrigerator that I see first thing every morning. It says, *I'm not in a hurry.*

12

Mountains of the Mind

Every one of us has had the experience which we have not been able to explain—a sudden sense of loneliness, or a feeling of wonder or awe in the face of the universal vastness... we have had a fleeting visitation of light like an illumination from some other sun, giving us in a quick flash an assurance that we are from another world, that our origins are divine.

A.W. Tozer, *The Pursuit of God*

...The four to five hours of marching, the hardly-ever-adequate let alone satisfying and tasty food, the often pathetic resting and overnight shelter conditions—these alone were sufficient, on a protracted itinerary, to wear out the bravest and the strongest among the pilgrims.

A description of Medieval Pilgrimage from
William Melczer, *The Pilgrim's Guide to
Santiago*

THERE IS A SAYING that the Camino Frances is broken up into three distinct stages: the physical, the mental, and the spiritual, each corresponding to a distinct portion of the Way. I had encountered the physical stage—and its challenges—my very first day, crossing the Pyrenees mountains, but they continued as I walked an average of 25 kilometers per day, through rain and snow, with blisters, sore feet and fatigue, to Burgos. That took me twelve days.

The mental stage began after I left Burgos and began my ten-day trek across the Meseta to the Irago mountains, the location of Cruz Ferro, which at over 1,500 meters is a literal and spiritual high point of the pilgrimage. I was looking forward to it. I had felt fed by the solitude and the quiet of the vast plains. But towards the end of the Meseta, in the region of Tierra de Campos, came a day of mental and spiritual endurance that wasn't mentioned as such in the guidebooks. By the end it felt every bit as significant a challenge as climbing the Pyrenees—I had to scale a mountain inside my head.

The challenge began when I came to a crossroads in the small town of Calzada de Coto. I had passed through Sahagun, the traditional "halfway" point of the Camino an hour earlier. The sky was hazy, the sun only making occasional appearances. Sahagun is a very ancient Camino town, famous, in fact, and is worth a longer visit. I just stopped long enough to look at one of the ancient churches and photograph some of the adobe and wooden structures. I wanted to continue on towards my destination for the day. On my way out of town I came across a flock of hundreds of sheep coming into town on the Camino. I had to step aside to let them pass.

Calzada de Coto is a crossroad of major highways. I had been walking parallel to one of them, the N-120, as I crossed the Meseta. Calzada is also a point where the walker has to choose between two routes; the southerly one runs alongside the busy highway and through more villages with services. The more remote, northerly one, was recommended by my guidebook and follows an ancient Roman road, the Via Trajana, to Reliegos, a distance of 25 kilometers. The sole stop is the small village of Calzadilla de los Hermanillos ("Road Town of the Little Brothers"), about eight kilometers down the road.

I crossed the highways and found an open café where I ordered a coffee and pastry while I pondered what to do next. The southerly route was more populated; indeed, most of my fellow pilgrims already told me they wanted to walk that way. The northerly route, the recommended one, seemed more of a challenge. Besides, I also had had enough of walking along monotonous, busy highways. In the summer this stretch can be extremely hot and many pilgrims who have taken it swear they wouldn't do it again, but it was still springtime for me, and the sun was not hot, even when the sky was clear.

I looked around; there were no other pilgrims. Out on the road, I saw no one, neither in front nor behind. I didn't like the indecision. Perhaps I could sense some "inner sign" for direction? None came. I finished my coffee and decided to go for the challenge.

The Via Trajana is known as one of the best sections of reconstructed Roman roads in all of Spain; it linked the gold mines of Galicia with Rome itself. Trees have been planted more recently alongside part of the road, but most of it is a vast, featureless plain, the red, dirt road straight, flat and dull. I had read that in the Middle Ages pilgrims became so disoriented here that they, "lost all sense of direction." Seeing no one ahead and no one behind, I understood. There was nothing along that stretch, except a large country home, with a sign saying *Coto Privado* or "private hunting reserve." After an hour, I came to a pilgrim shelter among a stand of trees, where I stopped to air my feet and eat a snack. A young woman passed by, the only person I had seen since leaving Calzada. She didn't stop.

I arrived in Calzadilla early afternoon and the town was indeed remote and small. I passed by a private albergue and then on to the parochial albergue in the center of the village; there were already two other pilgrims there ahead of me, a young man and young woman, he from Austria, she from Romania. They had met along the way and were now a couple, and they would be the only people staying there with me. The place had no heat, save a woodstove in the middle of the dining area and the young Austrian was struggling to keep it going. The hospitalera was friendly, but spoke only French and Spanish and we struggled to understand each other. Fortunately for me, the young Romanian woman spoke both Spanish and English, and she translated for us. After my usual arrival routine—a shower, laundry and nap—I searched the village for a tienda, where I bought food for the next day. When dinnertime arrived the hospitalera told me that the only open restaurant in the village was in the other albergue—called the Via Trajana— and I headed there, expecting to eat alone. Fortunately, I was joined by two young women, both doctors, one British, one American, the latter the same one who had saved me with her headlamp weeks before as we left Zubiri—I had not seen her since. We enjoyed a pilgrim supper and delightful conversation that stretched on quite late, until I glanced at my watch and said "good-night" abruptly, recalling the warning of the hospitalera that the doors would be closed and locked at 9:00—or was it 10:00?—with no entry allowed after that. I raced down the street to the albergue and, luckily, the doors were still open. I got myself ready for sleep and soon climbed into my sleeping bag for the night, in the very cool, and very quiet albergue.

I was up by 6:00 the next morning, my sleep fitful in anticipation of the day's walk. I hadn't realized when I had chosen this route just how remote and isolated I would be. The first stretch that day would be 17 kilometers, just as remote and desolate as the afternoon before. Ahead of me there were no mountains to climb; the challenge would be the remoteness, the loneliness. The mountains were in my *head*. And on top of it, the weather forecast looked doubtful, with overcast skies predicted. Might it rain? What would it be like walking so alone, with no villages, towns or snack stands along the Way? How well marked was the path? Might I get lost? I recalled how when I had previously missed the yellow arrows, there was often someone to call me back to the route. Not this day…

I ate a small breakfast: slices of a baguette, an apple and a cup of instant coffee. The hospitalera watched me prepare my coffee, murmuring to me first in French, then in Spanish her shock—genuine shock—that I was not warming the skim milk before I put it in my coffee. The young couple had not yet stirred, so the two of us ate mostly in silence, except for my paltry attempts at understanding her Spanish and French.

This was not the first time I would walk this far with no services; a few days before, upon leaving Carrion de los Condes, I had walked a similar 17-kilometer stretch. That day I had done it in the company of others; I had seen dozens of pilgrims before and behind me; but *this* day it would be just me and the road.

I finished my coffee, then packed, scoured my sleeping

bunk one more time for stray items, then shouldered my pack and left the warm lights of the albergue and headed westward out in the cold, dim dawn. The village was dead-quiet. I saw no one awake and since the windows were all shuttered, I saw no lights. In minutes I passed the last houses and then paused on the edge of the village to take in the vast horizon stretching in front of me.

I had started out alone many days before, but never quite like this. A blue and yellow scallop shell marker pointed me toward a blacktop road leading out of town, the sole assurance that I was heading along the correct route. Above were thick, gray clouds; they felt heavy and deepened my anxiety. Farther to my right they broke apart and I could see the in early light the snowy peaks of the Cantabrian mountains, 50 kilometers to the north. I stopped to take a picture of them; then I turned around to take one last shot of the village.

In theory, I knew others would be coming behind me. Civilization was out there—I could see the train in the distance—but I couldn't see the cities or towns. Some words of Bolitx came to mind: "I feel very small here, a tiny speck, unnoticed…" I love solitude, but this morning it felt mysteriously heavy. I humorously thought to myself, that if I became injured (and how could I, on this straight, flat stretch?) *at least the two doctors will be coming along, at some point* —and one of them was an ER doctor!

After 15 minutes the dim lights of Calzadilla were far behind me. In the distance I saw a teenage boy at a cross-road, book-bag on his back. His family farm was a kilometer to the north. He was the last person I would see for the next three hours.

After another 20 minutes, the blacktop road came to an end as I crossed another rural highway. Signs pointed to villages in each direction, but each were too far away to see. Irrigation pivots sat unused in the fields far to my left; in a ditch along the road I saw an abandoned computer monitor and a hubcap; heaped in a field was a pile of smooth, brown stones, picked from the fields: all signs of civilization. A drainage pond was filled with broken reeds. The marker for the Camino was ahead of me, a yellow arrow and a scallop shell.

A large road sign said, *Calzada Romana.* This was indeed a Roman Road, straight and flat, its sides slowly converging until they met at the horizon. Beyond the same horizon—directly west—I could also now see a small, faint line of snow-topped mountains, the ones I would have to cross over. Those were a long way away.

A kilometer to the south, I saw a high-speed train pass; another sign of civilization. My next stop—Reliegos—was still out of sight. I heard only my footsteps—a familiar "scritch, scritch" on the dirt road—and the click of my poles in rhythm. The Way markers were located on posts, about every kilometer. They were a comfort; they assured me that I was on the right way, though there was in reality no way I could get off-track—no forks, no junctions in the road, just desolate farmland.

Another hour passed and the clouds thinned and the sun shone behind me; my shadow fell straight down the road ahead—I was going the right direction, at least. Leon, Astorga, the mountains, Santiago: all to the west. Nevertheless, the total solitude, in the midst of this featureless expanse, was starting to get inside my head. I was used to walking *towards* something: the next village, or hill, or stand of trees, even just a house alongside the road. But here, there was nothing; no way to mark my progress, nothing to approach. Just… nothing. I felt profoundly alone, the only familiar thing was my shadow. I tried not to think about it too much.

Then after about 11 kilometers of this—over two hours —the dirt road angled toward the railroad track, nearly coming to it, but when I came alongside the tracks there was no crossing and I was certain that I was not supposed to cross them anyway, but walk parallel to them. Surveying my surroundings, I noted that a bulldozer had scoured the earth in a circle, obliterating the road. A deep drainage ditch crossed my path westward. I was bewildered; the Way had disappeared. There were no markings anywhere, no yellow arrows, no signposts. I couldn't cross the ditch and I knew I shouldn't go to my left and cross the tracks—there was no roadway on the other side either. I recalled how Medieval pilgrims had been so bedeviled in this vast *campos* that they had lost their way; now I understood. I walked in a circle for a few minutes, surveying the scene. A faint path—*perhaps it was the Camino*—appeared to head off to my right, skirting the drainage ditch. I looked back for other pilgrims, but saw no one and there was still no one ahead of me. Seeing no other options, I followed the faint path, uncertainly, seeing no clear markings for the Camino and eventually found myself diverging from the railroad, until it was a few hundred meters away to my left.

It was ten uneasy minutes until I came across a familiar Way marker and felt deep relief. In retrospect, the route should not have been so hard to figure out. I knew that my anxiety was irrational, but the vast emptiness, the desolation and the prolonged solitude had messed with my thinking.

Another kilometer and I encountered a farm shed, graffiti on its walls, and trash strewn about. A pair of abandoned hiking boots sat perched on a pile of bricks. I turned to look behind me—there was still no one. I sat down on the edge of the road to rest and removed my shoes and socks to air my feet. I pulled out an apple and a banana to eat. I heard only the birds, and the faint sound of traffic on the distant highway; the wind was quiet. *How much farther?*

A couple more kilometers—I'd been walking now for three hours and knew that Reliegos must be close—I passed a tractor with a trailer full of hay. Next to it were high mounds of freshly-dug potatoes. Signs of civilization! A little farther I came upon *bodegas,* wine cellars dug into the hillside and after that a cemetery and then finally the town. I was ready for my second breakfast and café con leche and some good conversation with someone—anyone!

I knew Reliegos was old—a town was there as early as 916 A.D. and before that it was a place where three Roman roads converged. (I imagined the thousands of Legionnaires walking through there!) But when I came into town I didn't find any Romans—I didn't find *anyone.* The cafés were closed and the houses' windows shuttered. No shops open, nothing. I was more than disappointed, I was mildly ticked-off. Where was everyone? This reminded me of the day weeks earlier when I approached Cirauqui in the mid-morning and had found it shuttered. This was one of the strange mysteries of Spain...

To my relief, I caught sight of a woman with a pack and poles and I walked towards her. Reliegos was where the southerly route—the one I had not chosen way back at Calzada de Coto—joined the Via Trajana and she had come into town that way. I was just happy to see another person. After greeting her with *"Buen Camino, hermana,"* I realized she spoke English, was in fact from Australia and was also looking for a café or a tienda. Her name was Narelle. She said that she also had found nothing so far and was equally frustrated and confused. After talking for a few

minutes, and looking at our guide books, we went separate
ways, to search the town in opposite directions.

More minutes passed; I found nothing open and came
across no one. This was really strange... Looking at my
guidebook, I realized that Mansilla, my destination for the
day, was six kilometers away and so reluctantly decided to
head there. Food and coffee would just have to wait.

The tree-lined path to Mansilla paralleled a quiet, car
road. Ahead I caught sight of Narelle sitting on a bench,
adjusting her shoe. She was just getting up as I approached
and we walked together for the next hour. I told her that I
had failed to find anything open, but Narelle had found a
small *mercado* and had bought chocolate and nuts. Sensing
that I was hungry, she pulled them out and shared them
with me. She also shared her story: she had started in St.-
Jean, leaving around the same time as me; her husband was
going to join her in ten days, in Sarria. What a coincidence!
My wife was also going to join me in Sarria, on the same
day. They might, in fact, even arrive on the same bus. I got
his name—Peter—and told her I would mention it to Jane.

Suddenly I forgot about hunger and frustration and
enjoyed the walk into Mansilla, swapping more stories about
our walk and about our blisters. (Hers had gotten so bad
that she'd stopped for a few days.) The Camino worked its
magic on me—I was glad to talk to a person, and my mood
was bolstered, even without caffeine. The central plaza of
Mansilla was, to my relief, alive with people and activity, and
open shops. Narelle and I parted ways—she going on to a
hotel and I to one of the municipal albergues. I told her that
I would look for her in Sarria, as I turned and headed off.

Hours later, showered, rested and now having a sandwich and a beer in a café, I wrote in a letter home:

They say that the first part of the Camino is a physical challenge—training the body to walk long distances, over hills and mountains, coping with aches and pains and blisters.

They say the second part—the flat and open Meseta —is an inner challenge. It involves hours of unchanging landscapes with endless sky. The pilgrim now turns inward. So it has been for me.

And the biggest challenge was yesterday and today, walking 25k along an old Roman Road, without another person in sight. I do enjoy solitude, but this was extreme. The only break was a small town where I stayed last night. I set off this morning at first light and under heavy clouds and for four hours saw no one. ..Even for the Camino this is unusual. I admit I was finally glad to come into a village, though ironically it was shuttered! I don't know where the Spaniards go on Monday mornings...

I have read the early "Desert Fathers" and of the early Irish *peregrinos* who sought the solitude of the desert. They were called the "The Athletes of God" and now after going through some of it myself I think I now really understand the term. Today was an inner workout.

Tomorrow on to Leon and after that, more mountains. It will feel like home.

I reflected yet later on this experience, and the utter desolation that I had felt, in conjunction with the lack of any "sign" about which way I should have gone. I recalled that sometimes God's gift to us is this type of desolation of spirit, an emptiness, a lack of God's presence. It is a mystery, but it also points to the significance of how often God *is* present, but we fail to look for that presence. For me, it took a day of walking in near-complete solitude—and near desolation—to learn to appreciate that, and how small we are in this vast universe.

PART IV

Crescendos

13

Mountains of the Spirit

...the path that follows the Milky Way (La Vía Láctea, in Castellano) has a history of millions of feet walking the same path, the very soul of all those people impregnates the earth that we all walk on during the Camino, as we too leave something of ourselves "out there" on the Camino, a tear, blood stains, screams on the mountain top etc. The very trees, rocks and plants felt our presence, heard our laughter, listened to our sobbing in the loneliness...

Mark Donovan Rodriguez

I LEFT the Meseta when I began the long and gradual climb to Monte Irago. My destination that day was the village of Rabanal, 1,150 meters in elevation. Seven kilometers beyond it is the *Cruz de Ferro* (Iron Cross) which, at 1,400 meters, is highest point on the Camino Frances. With its ancient stone cairn, it is one of the spiritual high points along the Way.

While I had enjoyed the solitude of the Meseta, the walk

to and through the cities of Leon and Astorga had become monotonous. Don't misunderstand—both cities were magnificent. Leon had its charming, old city center, its Roman walls and dramatic, light and airy cathedral. Astorga, perched on a hill, though much smaller, had its own gorgeous cathedral and bishop's house. I experienced warm hospitality and enjoyed pilgrim masses and blessings in each. Yet the approach to each city had been long, through dull industrial corridors, crossing busy highways into the cityscape. I longed for the small towns, the slower pace of the countryside. The two-day walk between the cities had taken me through more dreary towns, along straight and flat dirt paths that paralleled the highway; some of the villages and truck stops along there reminded me of the soulless sprawl of the U.S. more than the charm and magic of Spain. Only when I reached the cobblestoned streets of Hospital de Orbigo, 16 kilometers from Astorga, did the road break away from the highway, making twists and turns along an undulating and more inviting landscape.

Now I had left Astorga and was beginning to climb, very slowly at first. The landscape was arid, reminding me of the high deserts of the western U.S., with olive groves and scrub trees interspersed by oases of green. The dusty dirt road was tinged with red, the tiny villages featured narrow church towers topped by stork nests. I was going to miss those fabulous birds, with their long beaks and broad wingspans. Like the elusive cuckoos—always heard, but never seen—they were a fixture of the Meseta. This region was home to the Maragato, an insular group of people with uncertain origins, who may be the last surviving descendants of the Moors who once ruled Spain. Their houses are made of stone, with slate roofs, though a few have thatch. Neglected and fallen-down after the decline in the Camino, these villages are now being rebuilt and restored to their earlier charm. I chose to stop in the beautiful village of Rabanal, home to the albergue Guacelmo, named after a medieval monk who had founded several hospitals in the region.

I had read in several books that the Benedictine monks who serve the church in Rabanal chant vespers each evening, followed by a pilgrim's blessing. I didn't want to miss it and had marked it months earlier in my guide book. The albergue Guacelmo, run by the British Confraternity of St. James, was formerly the 12th century Hospital de San Gregorio. The monks, to my disappointment, were absent that day; there would be a vespers, but no chanting. The albergue, on the other hand, had been recently remodeled and was the cleanest, brightest and most beautiful that I stayed in during my journey. Our hospitaleros were a British couple who made us feel at home: helping with our laundry, building a cozy fire in the common room and gathering us for tea and spirited conversation in the late afternoon. The mountain air was refreshing and the vistas, were gorgeous, after several hot, dull days walking the last of the Meseta. And while the mountains were higher and drier than the Alleghenies that I view from my deck, I felt at home.

At this point it's difficult to conceive of any particular moment as climactic; just being on the journey was all a pilgrim could want. Each moment was so alive. This is the thing about walking the Camino: each moment is to be enjoyed, each destination to be anticipated, with a few especially anticipated. Cruz de Ferro was one of those, but so also was Rabanal.

After a blissful night's sleep in the mountain air, I headed out the next day for Cruz de Ferro. Located near the high point in the pass at Monte Irago, the cross is mounted on top of a thick pole (think telephone pole), stuck deep into a cairn (rock pile). Its origin is obscure, though the Celts often marked significant locations with cairns. The Romans may have continued the tradition, tossing a rock on top of the pile to appease the God Mercury, the god of merchants, travelers and transporters of goods. In modern traditions, pilgrims carry a stone from home to lay on the pile, perhaps representing a life's burden they want to shed. I knew some of those who laid aside momentous life burdens as they passed there. For many, this place and the tradition of leaving a rock or some other memento was, next to arriving in Santiago, a literal and figurative high point of their pilgrimage.

The early morning air was crisp and refreshing. The way up the narrow dirt path was lined with mounds of heather blooming in magentas and purples, hedges of prickly yellow gorse bush and thickets of Spanish broom, a green shrub with long, thin branches. Over low stone walls, I could see the mountains in the distance, covered in pines, their peaks draped in snow. I paused at several large stone water foun-tains—spring-fed pools, really—imagining them as places of welcome relief for tired pilgrims during the hot summer. The wind lightly rippled their surfaces as it reflected the beige stone and the surrounding mass of slumbering brown foliage against a bright blue sky. At this altitude, the trees were still barren, their branches lacing like spider webs reaching upwards. I felt an aura of mystery as my steps carried me upward. Maybe the cross was a special, spiritual summit, but the way up was already deeply tinged with holiness.

I walked about an hour to Foncebadón, a small, broken-down village, now being restored. I stopped for my "second breakfast" there and a pilgrim named Tim, now on his third Camino, told me that he hardly recognized it, it was so "developed." Along the side of the road were tall poles, striped at the top, put there to mark the way over the pass in deep winter, an ancient tradition that is still maintained.

When I arrived mid-morning at Cruz de Ferro, I found it covered with numerous make-shift memorials; photos, letters, poems, ribbons, stones with writing or initials on them, necklaces, all heaped on the pile or hanging on the pole. A few other pilgrims were there ahead of me, standing quietly, taking pictures, some praying. I took off my pack and set down my poles.

I had not brought a stone from home; instead, I brought a small Chesapeake Bay oyster shell, smooth and white. The day before, as I neared Rabanal, I had picked up one of the numerous, smooth brown stones that laid beside the road, tucked it into my pack as an extra offering to lay on the pile.

I stooped to lay down both. To my surprise, I was hesitant to let them go; they had become my companions along the way. For weeks I had absent-mindedly rubbed the oyster shell in my pocket and had grown used to its presence. The brown stone—so common, so banal in its original setting—now looked elegant and polished upon the cairn. I studied them in their new setting and imagined others who would look at them in the future; I would have to leave them and their beauty behind. I also spontaneously removed a "Pray for Peace" pin from my jacket and used it to tack a copy of my "pilgrim's prayer" to the pole, a gift to the Camino and to some unknown pilgrim in the future. I took time to look at the photos and notes tacked to the pole, mementos of other pilgrims. One caught my interest: a 20-year sobriety medal from AA. I later found out it had been left there by my friend Paul, one of several recovering alcoholics that I got to know and respect along the way. He and Lauri had passed through there just the day before and I felt was still walking with them.

The place had a sacred feel to it; I imagined the ancient Celts who had started the cairn, the Romans who had tossed their rocks on it, then all the pilgrims over the centuries who had passed the spot, as well as all the modern ones who had left something on it. I looked at some of the poems and photos attached to the pole and reflected on them; photos of loved ones lost, parents, children, spouses; they were part of the pilgrim community, same as me. We were together, just passing at different points in time. Santiago was our goal. But here, high in the mountains, with only the wind to be heard, was an equally "holy place," a focal spot, consecrated not by the bones and relics of a saint, but by the losses, the emotions, the grief, the triumph, the expressions of hope of a common humanity. I knew that for some, just reaching this spot was a celebration itself. Here the bond was not the destination, but the journey, an appropriate holy place for a walk that is as much about the journey as it is about the destination.

I was there only half an hour, but it seemed much longer. I discreetly took pictures, watching others (including fellow pilgrim friends Pam and Kathe) as they took their moments atop the cairn. The sky turned overcast; I enjoyed the serenity of the moment.

There are some who find Cruz de Ferro the peak of their experience. For me it was but one of many crescendos yet to come: the mountain pass at O Cebreiro, meeting my wife in Sarria, entering Santiago. I thought back to the feeling of exhilaration on my first day when I reached the pass in the Pyrenees; that had been one of those crescendos. The high points were important, but the descents off the heights, and the quiet days in between, was where most of the music of the Camino was played.

I re-shouldered my pack and picked up my poles, which I was going to need as I picked my way gingerly down the rock-strewn path into the Bierzo Valley, thinking to myself as I walked down the mountain, *it's a great day to be alive.*

14

Receiving the Camino

I know when the world feels anything less than miracu-
lous to me, I'm probably not paying attention.

Carrie Newcomer, *the beautiful not yet*

THE BEST EXPERIENCES on the Camino aren't
orchestrated. They are the unexpected encounters with
friends in cafés, the sandwiches, cookies and apples shared
at a picnic bench, the cups of coffee discovered on sleepy
mornings, the stranger with an amazing story to tell. By my
fourth week, I'd experienced enough of them that I should
have seen one when it was coming.

It was still early morning when I overtook my friends
Pam and Kathe as we approached the beautiful town of
Villafranca del Bierzo.[1] The Bierzo Valley, about 40 kilometers wide, lies between two mountain ranges (Monte Irago is
in the first) and pilgrims have to cross over both before
entering Galicia, where Santiago de Compostela lies. The
region has its own microclimate, excellent for growing fruit
and grapes and I experienced its delights. Spring was at its

peak as I passed through, with orchards of cherry in brilliant white blossom surrounding row after row of grapes. Villafranca is at the western end of the valley, at the confluence of the Rio Burba and the Rio Valcarce. The Camino Frances follows the Valcarce westward up to the O Cebreiro pass and into Galicia.

At the entrance to Villafranca lies the ancient Iglesia de Santiago, begun in 1186 A.D. In the Middle Ages, pilgrims who were too sick to go any farther could enter the church via the north portal, the Puerta de Perdón, and receive the same indulgences and forgiveness of their sins as they would if they had reached Santiago de Compostela. I'd read that there were intricate and well-preserved carvings above the Puerta and I lingered there for several minutes to take photographs of them, reminding myself, "I'm not in a hurry." Pam and Kathe walked on while I paused longer to look at the carvings and find the best angles for pictures. Satisfied that I had taken plenty of good shots, I continued down a paved path that descended to the center of town, intent on catching up to them.

Going only a few meters, I was passing the Albergue Fenix when the driver of a compact station wagon stopped, rolled down his window and motioned to me. He was one of several porters who carry backpacks for pilgrims to their next lodging. He had loaded up and was about to pull out, when he put on his brake, shut off the engine and climbed out. He started talking to me rapidly in Spanish and I didn't understand what he was saying, nor could I understand what he was motioning for me to do. Seeing that I didn't understand, he gently took hold of my shoulders and spun me 90 degrees, guiding me toward the doorway of the albergue, where he insisted I pull off my pack. I was still baffled and slightly resistant as he pushed me towards the door of the dining area, tugging at my pack and poles at the same time. I was suspicious, confused and defensive, all at once. What was going on?

Villafranca del Biezo with the Iglesia de San Francisco in the center, which according to legend was founded by Francis of Assisi on his way to Santiago

I reluctantly complied, dropped my pack, though I still couldn't figure out why or where he was pushing me. He opened the door of the dining area, ushered me in, and there I figured out his intent: there had been too much food laid out for breakfast and much of it was left over. He told me in Spanish that I was to eat whatever I wanted: it was *gratis* or free. I surveyed the dining area and saw laid out a feast: eggs with various cheeses and roasted peppers, toast, jam, fruit, orange juice, coffee, pastries. A vision of a Heavenly Banquet was in front of me and he reiterated that it was all for free. The pilgrims had all gone and the left-over food would go to waste. My face broke into a wide grin and

I nearly broke out laughing. "Gracias, gracias!" I said, nodding my head in comprehension. He smiled back, waved his hand again over the food, then returned to his car.

I wasn't all that hungry, but knew that in an hour I would be, so I ate, taking my time, savoring each bite of the delicious food, until I sat back, stuffed. It was the best breakfast I'd had yet in Spain. Sitting alone in the dining room I mused once again at my good fortune, feeling foolish— embarrassed, actually— at my initial resistance. A passage from the Gospels slowly came alive: the parable of the Wedding Feast, where God is compared to a master preparing a great banquet, but those invited are too preoccupied with the busyness (and business) of their lives and decline the invitation. Disappointed, the Master instead invites the poor, the crippled, the blind, and the lame. There is still room so the master orders his servants to search even wider, the roads and the country lanes, to "compel" more people to come. I saw myself as someone who was "compelled" to come in to the feast.

I can't say that there was a single "most important" lesson that I learned along the Camino; there were far too many to list only one. Likewise, there was not a single incident that stood above the others. But if there was one incident that encapsulated what the Camino means, it was the one that day in Villafranca del Bierzo: Life is offering us a feast, if only we will lay down our suspicions and our fears and *receive* it. On pilgrimage, it is referred to as "receiving the Camino." I was being offered a feast, I didn't know it and I resisted receiving it.

How often in life do we resist a feast that is laid out for us? How often do we have plans and miss the feast? This meal was a metaphor for the entire Camino, for life. There is so much out there for us, but we are content to miss it. We have to be in control of things, we have to follow a schedule, have to hurry along to the next appointment, the next task, the next item on our mental to-do list. Meanwhile, there are feasts waiting for us. The best experiences I had on the Camino were when things didn't go as I'd planned, but experiences which, if allowed, would become normal. They are gifts—moments of grace.

My youngest daughter asked me later that day in a message if I was learning anything new. I thought of my experience that day as I answered her. "I'm not sure if I'm learning anything new... just re-learning a lot of things I knew before... I'll put it this way: you can't teach an old dog new tricks, but you can teach an old dog his old tricks."

THE NEXT DAY I had an opportunity to give back.

I had walked up the Valcarce Valley as far the village of Trabadelo, about ten kilometers after Villafranca and got a bed at Casa Susi, a new albergue. The Rio Valcarce runs behind it and I soaked my aching feet in the ice-cold water for as long as I could stand it—it helped relieve my sore feet. At our communal meal that night I met Jeff and Kate, from northern Virginia, and Nerida and Jess, two women from Australia. Jeff, an Episcopal priest, was on sabbatical; he and Kate had started five days earlier in Leon and were still getting used to the pace. The Australians had walked all the way from St.-Jean and were expecting to arrive in Santiago within a week. We talked at length about what we hoped to do once we arrived in the city and about whether or not we intended to continue onto Finisterre. We tentatively agreed to meet for supper at the end of the journey and celebrate.

I was up before light the next morning, and enjoyed an

unusually hearty breakfast—muesli, fruit, bread, juice and coffee. I had a shorter distance to go that day, 22 kilometers, and not being in a hurry—my new normal!—I took time to write postcards and record the previous days' experience in my pocket journal. My pilgrim companions got up and left while I tarried, making me the last to leave.

I had not gone more than a kilometer before I came across a red raincoat in the path: an expensive, high-tech jacket whose owner would surely be missing it. Nerida and Jess were about a half kilometer ahead of me; I could just make them out. *This probably belongs to one of them,* I thought to myself. Figuring that I would overtake them, I looped it over the top of my pack and continued. That section of the Camino follows an old highway; the new superhighway atop concrete piers carries swift traffic a hundred feet above. Concrete barriers separate pilgrims from the old road as it twists and curves through several small villages. Somewhere along there I lost sight of the women. I was sure they would be in one of the cafés that I was passing. As I went through each village, I asked about the two, showing the raincoat. No one said they'd seen them. Mildly perplexed, I carried the coat over top of my pack for the rest of the day, making the hot, steep and beautiful climb over O Cebreiro—the border of Galicia—in early afternoon. I stopped in the tiny town of Linares, perplexed that I still had the coat and had not encountered its owner. Where could they be?

The next morning was misty and I began my descent of the western side of the mountain, the fog thinning as I gradually descended deeper into Galicia. I came across Pam and Kathe in the café at Alto do Poio and asked them if they'd seen Jess or Nerida. They said they didn't even know them. I walked another ten kilometers before I gave up on finding the owners; I had passed scores of pilgrims along the way and by that point figured that I was most likely *ahead* of its owner and so decided on another tactic. At a steep point along the descending trail I came across a wide-open curve, and hung the raincoat prominently on a tree, figuring that the owners were still behind me and would see it. I blessed the coat as I left it, hoping it would be reunited with its owner, or if not, at least be useful to another pilgrim. I walked on towards my destination for the day.

That evening in Triacastela, Jeff approached me as we were eating supper in an outdoor café. Did you leave this raincoat along the trail? He held up the red coat. Astonished, I said, "Yes! How did you know?" The Camino has its own grapevine and he had heard from someone who had heard from someone else that I was looking for the owner of a red raincoat. "Jess texted me that she had lost her raincoat and asked me to look for it. I was coming down the mountain this morning, hoping I'd find you—and there was the raincoat, hanging on a branch! It was like magic... I'm going to let her know that I have it. She's a few villages ahead and we're going to meet in Sarria tomorrow. She'll be very relieved."

We all laughed at this turn of events and I smiled as I continued with my supper, thinking, *sometimes you make the Camino Magic yourself.*

Suseia y Ultreia: Onward and Upward

God is not just the source of beauty; God is beauty. That means beauty sits out of time and space, breathing into our world as an eternal whisper of our maker.

Makoto Fujimara, "A Conversation with Artist
Makoto Fujimura on Beauty, Mission, and
Culture Care"

WHAT TIME WAS IT? I didn't know. Where on the road was I? I didn't know. Time and space had lost relative sense; I was somewhere along the Camino and the morning sun was shining. The air was warm and delicious. The leaves were budding out on all the trees; the ferns unfurling their fiddleheads along the forest floor. Everywhere around me was beauty. That was all that mattered.

In actuality, I was in Spain, in Galicia, west of Triacastela, on my way to Sarria, 20 kilometers and a few hours away. It was Thursday, April 26, 2018, about 9:00 in morning, but as far as I was concerned, I might as well be in heaven.

The night before, something unexpected had happened. After a filling and satisfying supper with my friends Pam and Kathe and some others, we had gone to a Pilgrim Mass and blessing. As usual, it was in Spanish; I knew just enough of the liturgy and just enough Spanish to comprehend. There were around 20 people in attendance and I was sitting near the front and so was one of the first in line as we all came forward to receive the eucharist. As a respectful non-Catholic I learned long ago to approach the priest and, crossing my arms in front of my chest, bow for a blessing, instead of holding out my hand for the host. But it went differently that night. Approaching the priest, I bowed, leaned forward and... nothing. I looked up and the priest looked at me intently and motioned for me to take the Host. I did.

This affected me deeply. I had carried mixed emotions about the *very* Catholic nature of the Camino, knowing full well the ancient and medieval history of Spain, a history of conquests, wars, inquisitions, of colonialism. I cringed inwardly at the images of St. James the warrior, the "Matamoros," the slayer of Muslims. The Burgos Cathedral had many splendid side-chapels, each full of priceless artwork. As I pondered the golden retablos built in the 16th and 17th centuries, I could not help wondering if the gold had come from mines in South America, which had employed slave labor under brutal conditions. At the same time, I had felt drawn to the images of St. James the simple pilgrim and to the simplicity of the life of a pilgrim myself, thinking of the many millions who had walked along that Way over the centuries. My reservations never kept me from attending pilgrim Masses and services of blessing. This was a spiritual pilgrimage for me and I immersed myself in it. Yet, when the Eucharist came, my sense of being different, of not quite being fully accepted, was apparent, even if I completely understood and accepted it.

That simple gesture from that priest made me feel fully part of the Camino, of the community "of the centuries" who had walked this way. I was part of it and it was a part of me. This thought was with me that morning as I departed Triacastela, heading to Sarria.

I HAD MORE reasons to relish this incredible day. The next day was going to be a rest day and, best of all, Jane was going to meet me. If her flight and bus itineraries all worked out, we would walk together the last 113 kilometers to Santiago. I might have less solitude, but my loneliness for her and my family would be over. I would share with her about my experiences so far, and we would share together what was still to come. I walked in high anticipation, but first I had to experience *this* day. Tomorrow would be a wonderful reunion, but I needed to fully experience and appreciate THIS DAY.

I will always remember Galicia as green. Nearly 1,000 meters lower in elevation than the mountains, it was wetter, more densely forested and everything a lush green. The stone walls lining the roads had a different character from anything I'd seen so far; there were large narrow slabs set vertically into the ground, like a stone fence, lining the road. At each farmstead or home were the *hórreos*, narrow wooden granaries perched upon stone pillars with broad roofs, topped with the occasional cross, looking like a shrine.

Every day for the past month I had been consulting my guidebook before I left my albergue, noting the names of towns, distances and any possible places to stop for coffee or second breakfast. But this day was different. I glanced at the book, thought about how far I had to go and then stashed the book in my pack. *This* time I was going to simply walk and enjoy, blissfully unaware of where I might be.

It took me a month of walking, but this was the day that I had been looking for, without even knowing it, a day to relish, a day to simply BE. Walking, I took in each moment, each sight, each bird song, each stone and each tree. Sparrows alighted on the path ahead of me, chirped and hopped along the road, as if showing me the way to go. Inside came a deep peace; my mind was fully alert to experience whatever came next. I existed in a sense of wonder, expectant in a calm sort of way—just walking the Camino was now my life. Since I knew neither the time, nor where exactly where I was along the path, it was as if time and space didn't matter.

It was a gorgeous day for picture taking. I stopped to take a particular shot of sheep pastures and hills to the south. Every few feet the angle got better, or the light got better, so I stopped, re-framed and focused it, and took another shot. Then I just stopped—it hit me that there was no way I was going to get the ultimate shot. The calculating, the thinking, were distracting me from the moment. I already had over 2,000 photos from the Camino. I decided that I would commit this time, this place, to memory and recall forever that it was beautiful. No need to *record* it, except in my memory; no need for another picture. I put the camera away for the time being, along with the guidebook. Thoreau said, "A man is rich in proportion to the number of things which he can afford to let alone." I was rich in scenery, I would be rich in memory; I could "let it alone;" I could do without another picture. I just wanted to drink it all in, let the moment saturate me. And it did.

I dug into my pocket and pulled out my sheet of prayers —I had them memorized, so I really didn't need it—and as I prayed my morning office, I stopped when I got to this verse in Psalm 37

Let the dawn bring news of your faithful love,
For I place my trust in you.
Show me the road I must travel
for you to relieve my heart.

I repeated the sentence, "show me the road that I must travel for you to relieve my heart," several times. This had been in my prayers for a long time: five years? Ten years? I had prayed it through difficult times of work, through the many pressures of family life, through my many moves, through my inner dis-comfort and mis-fit in society. Who was I? Why was I so different? Where did I fit? What road, what path through life was the way I was supposed to follow? Up until then, I wasn't certain.

Yet at that moment, in prayer, it hit me: this was the road. *This was the road*, the Way, but more than the physical road, this was *Life itself.* Not just the walking, the outdoors, not just the culture: it was all of it wrapped together, having all the time I needed, not being in a hurry, not having any agenda. It was a day to be fully alive, a day I return to over and over in my memory. I knew right then that I should never forget this moment, this answer to prayer.

It was a gift of grace.

I could have only achieved it through walking the Way, especially this one, this time. It's a way of leaving the world and recovering your native sensitivities. It's not just me, either—pilgrimage does that to people. It's a scenario sustained by simple, ritual gestures in a historic framework that requires many kilometers and many steps—steps faithful to a promise, or to an aspiration. It's a determination to give the best of oneself, on a Way that is so much more than stages in an itinerary. It's an opportunity, a change, a dream, a comfort, perhaps, for a few days, a different way of being in a world that's different from the ordinary but still very real.

At the same moment that I stumbled upon this profound moment of grace, I stumbled across yet more Camino Magic: an old farmstead-turned-into-pilgrim-refuge, barn doors wide-open, a table set with fruit and pastries, surrounded by lounge chairs and couches, free-formed art painted on rocks and perched on the walls. Terra Luz. A pony-tailed young man named Simon asked me, did I want some coffee? "Coffee? Of course! Thank you," I replied. He disappeared inside and emerged a few minutes later with a delicious cup of espresso and a croissant on a plate. Other pilgrims were hurrying by, grabbing a banana or bottle of juice, but I had already shed my pack and poles and had sat down. I was in no hurry.

I asked about him: he was from Australia, he said, had walked the Camino, then decided to settle along it and had actually just arrived back to help at this place the day before. This was the first day it was open, his first day as a hospitalero. Serving pilgrims was his vocation, if not for his life, at least for now.

I thanked him for the coffee and croissant, and dropped some euros into the donation box. I lingered there longer, enjoying the flowers, the artwork, the atmosphere, then slowly gathered up my things and walked on to Sarria, another ten kilometers. I got my camera out again, but this time I took pictures of people: of pilgrims, of the locals, of pilgrims interacting with the locals. One old man sat in a chair in the shade alongside the road, "pilgrim-watching," I supposed. I pulled out the last of my "peace pins" and a "pilgrim's prayer" laid it them on top of a Way marker, an offering for some pilgrim following behind. I passed through more stone villages, passed cafés where pilgrims lounged over their second breakfasts. Time passed, but I was still not aware of it.

Simon, at Terra Luz

I arrived in Sarria in this state of mind, climbing its steep streets lined with shops and cafés, busy with throngs of new pilgrims. I ran into a couple from Canada, friends of a friend, who had been looking for me for weeks. We arranged to have supper together. My albergue for the night had not yet opened and so I sat on the grass with several others: Fred, Kathe, Pam, Jeff and Kate. Jess arrived and was happily reunited with her red raincoat and insisted that she buy me a beer that afternoon. I tipped my hat down over my eyes and laid back on the lawn and basked in the warmth of the air, the memories of the day, the magic of the Camino and the community of my fellow pilgrims. I thought about my upcoming day of rest, about the fact that Jane would soon be leaving on her journey to meet me. More than anything, I thought about the beauty of Galicia, the beauty of that day and recalled the famous words from Dorothy Day: "The world will be saved by Beauty."

PART V

Arriving

Walking two moons

The Camino is now something much more than a physical and mental challenge, more than something to check
off my life's list of 'to-do's' and more even than the
accomplishing of my personal goal to seek the help of a
grand old saint for the great cause of my life. This is now
life itself.

Kevin Codd, *To the Field of Stars*

I RESTED the next day in Sarria as I waited for Jane to
arrive.

I had loved this time of solitude and of sharing this
unique experience with other pilgrims, but without my
family, it always felt like part of me was missing. Ever since
we met back in college, Jane and I had become each other's
chief confidante and companion. At home, we garden and
cook together, growing much of our own food. In the
kitchen, we love to experiment with new recipes. We both
love to walk and to read; we share the same political and
spiritual values and have always supported each other's

interests. Of course, our greatest common interest is our six
kids and our grandkids.

Jane is full of energy. For her, home is a wellspring of
nurture and creativity. She experiments with fermented
foods and sprouted-wheat breads in her kitchen "laborato-
ry." She is a fiber artist and can easily spend hours in her
sewing room, designing and piecing quilts. She has a passion
for children, for mothers, for nutrition and healthy lifestyles
and is always learning something new and eagerly sharing
what she discovers with any interested child, parent or
neighbor. She had just recently become a *doula*, a birth
coach. She's also my biggest supporter and the best critic of
my writing.

Home is the womb of her abundant community, so she
seldom wants to be away as long as I do. She wanted to join
me on the last leg but encouraged me to pursue my dream
and start the journey from St.-Jean, solo. When I travel, I
immerse myself in the history and the culture of a place, its
geography, politics and food and when she's with me in our
travels, we share it together. On my own, I write letters and
call every few days. We were accustomed to my taking a
week away, alone, to walk, pray and meditate and so she was
used to greeting a "Russ" newly transformed by those experiences. The Camino, of course, took that to a whole new
level.

I was on an inner journey, a pilgrimage. We both knew
from the outset that it was going to be a life-changing experience. What would it mean to be separated during such a
significant time? There was a little bit of a tension within
her; when she arrived would she feel an outsider to my
experience?

For my part, I was just eager to be reunited with her

again, walking side-by-side, sharing this journey with my closest friend.

LIKE MY DAY IN BURGOS, I found it difficult to rest; I watched the crowds depart—my Camino friends among them—and felt the itch to be going, too. Yet this was also a day that I'd been looking forward to for weeks, so I contented myself by relaxing for two hours in a café, bringing my journal up to date and writing postcards. Jane was not arriving until late afternoon, so I strolled around town, shopped for equipment, found a delicious *pastelería* (pastry shop) and took photos. I moved out of the albergue and into a pensión, a private room in a small apartment building that was next to the bus station.

Walking the town, I couldn't help but notice the swarms of people. I'd heard that Sarria could be very crowded but this was more than that—it was overwhelming. To receive a Compostela, the certificate of completion, a pilgrim must walk at least 100 kilometers to Santiago. Sarria is 113 kilometers away and a convenient hub for mass transit and is thus the most popular place for pilgrims to begin. I wondered how that would affect my pilgrimage from here on.

I arrived at the bus station a few minutes before 5:00. A lot of connections had to work out on Jane's part: bus to the airport, flight to Frankfurt, another flight to Santiago, and a final bus to Sarria. It would take her over 24 hours. In my experience I knew how much could go wrong with any of those connections. A lot of alignment was required for both of us, actually. I had to think of the 700 kilometers I'd walked to

get to that very spot, on that very day, at that very *hour*, from
the French Pyrenees, through the river valleys of Basque country, across the vast Meseta, across more mountain ranges—all
in good time, with just a few small blisters, no other injuries. I
knew others who had fallen coming down the mountains, or
who had suffered tendinitis, or who were waylaid for days with
debilitating blisters. Some, in disappointment, had cut short
their pilgrimage. So much could have gone wrong and kept
either one of us from our much-anticipated reunion. I also
thought back to the surprising deep loneliness I had felt the
first morning of my walk and then how the mysterious energy
of the pilgrimage, the community with others, the hours in
quiet solitude, all had deepened God's presence and helped
filled the hole created by the natural longing for my family.

Jane kept in touch via text and I was relieved each time
another leg of the journey went without a hitch. The last
message reported that she'd boarded a full bus in Santiago,
bound for Sarria. I'd walked a month thinking of this day,
and in a few minutes, I would welcome her into my new
world.

Heading towards a bench to wait for the bus, I spied a
woman with long silver hair waiting. It was Narelle from
Australia, the woman I'd met in Reliegos ten days earlier,
where we had realized that our spouses would both be
arriving on *this* bus. We'd walked the same road for the last
ten amazing days, passing through Leon and Astorga, over
two mountain ranges… and all during that time had not
seen each other. We laughed at this fact as I took my place
on the bench next to her to wait for the bus, the excitement
in each of us building.

Five o'clock came and went; where was that bus? Five
minutes late… eight minutes… then suddenly around the
corner it appeared and pulled to the stop. The back door

opened and I tried not to be impatient as a line of slow-moving passengers, some of them pilgrims, began to disembark. Where was she? I peered anxiously through the crowd and then, finally—there! I hopped off the curb, gave her a kiss and a long hug and whispered thankfulness to God that she had arrived. The last people got off and it included Peter, Narelle's husband. We exchanged introductions and before we went separate ways, agreed to look out for each other as we headed towards Santiago. We walked the half-block to the pensión, where she was able to shed her pack. I knew she hadn't slept in 36 hours, but she was surprisingly alert and I was eager to show her around the town.

We climbed the main street in town, the Rúa Maior, passing shops, crowded outdoor cafés and restaurants, hotels and albergues and I pointed out some pilgrims I had met along the way. At 6:00 it was early for an authentic Spanish supper, but not too early for a pilgrim meal. We found a nice restaurant serving "genuine" peregrino fare, where we could sit over bowls of soup, loaves of bread and glasses of wine and finally catch up, face-to-face, after four weeks. There was so much to talk about, but after an hour and a half I could see that she was fading. I knew we would have the next ten days to talk all we wanted to, so after a delicious dessert of Spanish *flan*, we paid our bill and started the walk back down the *rúa* and the last half-mile to the pensión, falling gratefully into a comfortable bed and a good night's rest.

THE NEXT MORNING, Saturday, we were excited: Jane's first day on the Camino! We gathered all our belongings into our packs and headed down the four flights of stairs to the street. There was a light haze in the sky, but the weather was supposedly going to be spectacular. We had passes for breakfast at a café a block away and there I received my first shock of the day: the place was *packed*. We had to wait 20 minutes just to get attention at the bar and had to eat our Spanish breakfast of bread, coffee and orange juice standing. We headed back up the Rúa Maior, following the yellow arrows along the Camino. There were tremendous swarms as we departed town: packs of school children, tourist buses unloading "day walkers," and family groups on holiday. The number of pilgrims had jumped ten-fold. Jane and I were carrying seven kilo backpacks and poles; they were carrying water bottles and umbrellas. I had carried that pack on my back 700 kilometers over our weeks to get to this point. This was tourism, not a pilgrimage![1]

Until that moment I hadn't realized that we were heading out at the start of a long Spanish holiday weekend. Tuesday would be May Day, a holiday, and many people took that long weekend to walk this stretch of the Camino. It could be done in a little over four days (we were going to take six) and they would receive a coveted Compostela for their efforts.

In the first hours we came upon the 100-kilometer marker—we were counting down the last steps at this point —but at first each stop was crowded. At cafés, we waited to get into the bathroom and waited to get served at the counter. At one narrow choke-point, where the road became a narrow, single-file path between stone walls, I had to stop and wait my turn to pass through. "It doesn't feel like the Camino anymore," I told Jane. I had been warned this was coming, but the reality was worse than I imagined. The people walking near me no longer felt like fellow pilgrims, but more like competitors. What were we going to do?

We walked 20 kilometers to Portomarín, our destination

for the day. Just before town we came across tour buses picking up walkers to take them to their hotels. I was flabbergasted. We crossed the long bridge over the reservoir[2] and up a hill into town, where we hoped to find a room in an albergue. The first two we tried were full; we managed to find top bunks in a third. I had wanted Jane to experience an albergue, but this was not the best way to begin. Over supper we talked at length about what to do: the pilgrimage was supposed to be special, but at this rate it was going to become stressful. Reluctantly, we decided to do one thing I hadn't wanted to: we booked rooms for the following nights, all the way into Santiago. This would violate a principle of my pilgrimage, but it felt far worse to resent the crowds.

This turned out to be a relief and a wise decision.

Already the next morning we had a more relaxed attitude about the crowds and I became a whole lot less judgmental. We chose to walk a shorter distance, 19 kilometers, in order to get "off stage," meaning that we wouldn't be staying in the larger towns with the crowds. We stopped in the tiny hamlet of Portos—nothing there except our albergue—in early afternoon, where we had booked a room with six other pilgrims. There we met for the first time a young English woman, Sarah, who was walking with her mother. She had left St.-Jean the day before me and her mother had joined her in Sarria. Jane—who has never met a stranger—made friends with the two instantly. We had supper with them and talked about our experiences of the past month. The fact that so many people had someone meeting them—a relative, friend, or spouse—made Jane feel less like she was the only "newbie" pilgrim along the Way. The evening was rainy and a bit cool, so we sat by a fireplace and kept warm while we read books or continued to chat.

The next day was sunny, but by now we were so far *behind* the crowds that it felt like we had the whole Camino to ourselves. My critical spirit about the "touristagrinos" fell away and the delight of the pilgrimage returned.

While I had always wished that Jane could have gone the entire way with me, we were now spending all day walking together, with no agenda, no phones ringing, no appointments to get to—we had the luxury of time. Nothing to plan except where we would stop for coffee, or lunch. I had written numerous letters and emails home, and had spoken to her and other family members on the phone, but there was so much more she wanted to tell *me*. She shared news about friends and neighbors, about our children and grandchildren. I wanted to tell her more about the people I'd met, about the changes I felt come over me during the long days walking outdoors, much of it in solitude. I always struggled to be a good listener, often rushing people or finishing their sentences. Now I noticed that I wasn't practicing this bad habit. *I was no longer in a hurry*. The Camino had worked on me.

WHAT FOLLOWED WERE ENCHANTING DAYS. We passed *castrum*, the ancient hill-forts created by the Celts and taken over by the Romans. We passed farm villages with stone houses, tractors and barns, pastures with sheep and cattle. We met local farmers returning from their fields with wheelbarrows full of *berza*, tall cabbage stalks that are a staple in Galician soups. We walked sunken lanes with high, stone walls, lush in moss, ivy and ferns. Massive oak trees intertwined their branches overhead, and we felt like we walked through a green tunnel. At times the road was a stream bed and we had to step carefully along stepping stones. We passed through eucalyptus forests, with their commanding, intoxicating fragrance, the trees tall, with massive trunks. With the dampness and the stone walls and houses, we felt like we were in Ireland—and it made sense, since this is the Gaelic part of Spain. But we also joked at times that it felt like the enchanted forest in the *Wizard of Oz*.

Jane loves to talk to new people and she struck up conversations easily. We met still *more* people who had left St.-Jean around the same time that I had, but whom I had never seen. One couple—she was from Australia, he from California—had walked as far as I had and also complained about the sudden crowds. He was taking a year sabbatical, as I was, but he was 20 years younger, so he needed to head back to his work. We talked at great length about the excitement of approaching Santiago and wondered together how we would ever return to "normal" life after we were done.

Lighting the *queimada* in Salcedo

I was happily surprised that the closer we got to Santiago, the owners of the albergues and cafés—in spite of the crowds—seemed to be enjoying themselves as much as the pilgrims. One café we stopped at in Salceda gave us a chance to sample an old local custom, the *queimada*, an alcoholic drink set on fire, to "ward off evil spirits." Ours was laden with roasted coffee beans, which I supposed would keep us alert, as well as protected. The barrista in another café in that town fashioned portraits of his customers in their café con leche, carefully swirling the rich, brown coffee on the surface of the hot milk. He was so relaxed and having so much fun that he invited us to come on his side of the bar to try to fashion one of him. We enjoyed this town so much that we called it "the town where people forget to be unhappy."

JUST BEFORE DAWN on the first morning in May, I saw the moon setting directly ahead on our path, just outside of the town of Melide. This was always a good indicator that we were headed the right way. We had just two days more before the end of the pilgrimage. As I paused to take a picture, it occurred to me that I had seen the same thing before—exactly four weeks before—as I was leaving the town of Puenta La Reina just before dawn on the fifth day of my journey, 600 kilometers back. Then it hit me: I had been walking every day for a month. I had experienced and learned so much that it seemed like years. This road was now "life itself."

Simultaneously, a small feeling of melancholy came over me—the Camino was soon going to end. I was going to have to savor each moment from here on.

You did it!

Keep Ithaka always in your mind.
 Arriving there is what you were destined for.
 But do not hurry the journey at all.
 Better if it lasts for years,
 so you are old by the time you reach the island,
 wealthy with all you have gained on the way,
 not expecting Ithaka to make you rich.

Konstandinos Kavafis, *I will walk towards my Ithaka,*

IT WAS a warm sunny morning two days later as Jane and I entered Santiago de Compostela, the destination that I had been thinking about for the past five weeks—the destination that is the end of a journey I'd been thinking about for 20 years.

The walk that morning hardly seemed a walk at all, more a celebration than anything. Beginning just before sunrise in Lavacolla—a village ten kilometers from Santiago, where in the Middle Ages pilgrims stopped for ritual bathing in the river before entering the city—the sun came up behind us and together we followed our shadows. We made an obligatory stop about five kilometers out from the city center, on Monte de Gozo (Mount of Joy) known for nearly 900 years as the spot where pilgrims got their first glimpse of the towers of the Cathedral, their excitement and antici-pation nearing its peak. We stopped and looked at the modern monuments at the top of the hill and then glimpsed the towers with excitement ourselves—and thought of how medieval pilgrims must have felt. We got our picture taken, then descended an asphalt trail, the sun touching our backs. We crossed a pedestrian bridge over the highway, and dropped into the outskirts of the city, hitting asphalt, then cement sidewalk. I tucked my walking sticks into the side of my pack.

SANTIAGO IN MAY IS STUNNING, the trees leafed-out and flower beds in full bloom, the air delicious with their scents. Over its 500 miles, the Camino Frances goes through more than a half-dozen larger towns and cities and the entry to several of them was far from beautiful—industrial, dirty and noisy, with trucks and fast-moving car traffic. By contrast, Santiago was serene, quiet, pedestrian, the clean residential neighborhoods filled with appealing stone buildings. Even though the Cathedral was our goal, we were taking our time, savoring every moment, ignoring our feet, not even feeling the ground, like we were walking on air. Being in no hurry, we stopped for freshly squeezed *zumo naranja*, more café con leche and pastries. We took everything in, those final kilometers, as we gently climbed our way closer to the center. Our excitement was building as we glimpsed the towers of the Cathedral. The sidewalks had scallop shells embedded in them, to guide us towards our destination, but even without them we sensed where we were going. After five weeks of walking, I was *almost there*.

As we entered the old part of the city, with its narrow, twisting streets and high stone buildings, a line of pilgrims in front and behind us, I thought back to that first cool and rainy morning in St.-Jean, which now seemed so long ago. I recalled how I had begun my journey that gray day in the warmly-lit pilgrim office where the French volunteer had handed me my credencial and rubber-stamped it. I remembered how I paused to look down, running my finger over the inked image of a medieval pilgrim and read: St.-Jean-Pied-de-Port, 29/3/2018. The long-anticipated day of my departure—and my first stamp, on the top left corner of my credencial, the beginning.

I recalled how I had walked 50 meters down the narrow, ancient cobblestone street and stopped at the city gate, the Port de Maria. Directly out that gate is a bridge over the river Nieve and the start of the Camino Frances, the starting point not just for me, but for millions of modern and ancient pilgrims, a place not just of history but of hopes and dreams—spanning centuries. I had gotten a lump in my throat then as I had paused alone in the drizzly rain to take a photo of my foot as I went through the gate, crossed the bridge and headed out on my first kilometer.

Now, on my last kilometer, as Jane and I wound our way with the crowds through the streets of the medieval city center, I felt the same lump rise in my throat. I had long fantasized the moment that I would arrive, and here it was, a Thursday: five weeks to the day—almost to the hour— since I'd begun. Later that day I planned on going to the Pilgrim office and receiving my last stamp: Santiago, 3/5/2018.

While I had enjoyed the solitude of the Camino, had enjoyed the new friends that I had made along the way, it meant everything to have Jane by my side at that very moment. She had known me almost my entire adult life. She had known my hopes and wishes for this over the past decades, my longing for a pilgrimage, had patiently listened to me through my reading, my planning, my dreaming. She had even blessed me as I left, knowing I would not see her for over four weeks. But now she had been walking with me for six days, long enough for her to understand what it actually felt like to be a pilgrim. She had seen me off as I departed and she was with me now as I arrived.

We crossed the Plaza Cervantes and, turning a corner, found ourselves unexpectedly at the north side of the cathedral. I paused to take it all in: pilgrims streaming past, tourists pouring out of the cathedral, the crowds at vendors' stalls along the side of the street, the towers of the cathedral and the deep blue sky overhead. I wanted to walk more slowly; I passed the north entrance and descended the steps that led through a portal and out into the vast Praza de Obradoiro. That large plaza, facing the iconic western façade of the cathedral, is the place where pilgrims for centuries have gathered to enter the Portico de la Gloria, the western door of the cathedral.

As we went down the steps into the portal, I was arrested by something unexpected: a bagpiper. This being the Gaelic region of Spain, I should have known better. His music filled the portal and my own emotion welled up with it. I was arriving; the journey was coming to an end.

We passed the bagpiper and found ourselves entering the enormous plaza. All around were clumps of people, mostly sightseers at this time of the morning, but here and there were pilgrims with packs on their backs; gawking at the cathedral, getting their picture taken with it towering in the background.

As we headed towards the plaza center, a woman ahead of us waved with excitement. It was Narelle, who had arrived the day before. We were recognized and being welcomed!

Or not…

Still looking straight towards us, Narelle jumped up and down and shouted congratulations. A few feet away, I shouted back, "thank you," only to realize that she was not greeting us, but a couple of pilgrims just steps directly behind us, a young woman from Germany and her father. She ran past us and hugged them. I felt a bit awkward, even embarrassed, but as they turned back to us, a look of recognition came over her face and we both laughed. While her initial enthusiasm had been for someone else, she of course recognized us and then gave us a hearty hug and our own congratulations.

As we stood in the middle of the plaza, gazing at the cathedral, an American tour group and their guide came upon us. An older gentleman (older than me) began questioning us. When I told him that I had set out five weeks earlier and had walked the entire 500 miles on foot just to arrive at this spot, he looked as if I had just told him I'd flown to the moon. In awe, he asked to have his picture taken with us and began to tell his wife and others the amazing news of what I had just done. It seemed strange to me that he was unaware that so many millions of pilgrims had done what I had just done, but it didn't matter at that point; I became a celebrity, if only for the briefest of moments.

Peter and Narelle told us that if we could drop off our packs at our lodgings, we would be in time for the pilgrim mass which was to begin in a little over an hour. And would we like to meet them for it? We located our lodging on my phone's map and started off. Before leaving the plaza, though, I stopped and looked back once again at the cathedral, trying to say something through the lump in my throat. I pulled Jane aside and said, "we did it!" She looked me and said, "No, *you* did it!"

I had done it. I had arrived. I had walked 500 miles, but it was not about the cathedral. The cathedral, in all its magnificence, was just the end point that signified for me the *journey*. And the journey had been the fulfillment of a *dream*; and now the dream, the journey, the cathedral: all of it was real. All of it.

AFTER UNLOADING our gear at our nearby pensión, we headed back to the cathedral. The northern transept was reserved for pilgrims and we moved our way forward to squeeze into a seat next to Narelle and Peter and the German pair. The central nave, to our right, was packed with what I assumed were tourists. Looking around I could see familiar faces of other pilgrims that I had encountered over the past five weeks. Fred, in shorts, waved and smiled to me from several rows back. Carl, whom I had first met at the train station in Bayonne, had arrived just the day before and was sitting in thoughtful meditation behind Fred. I waved a greeting to more people I knew. I wanted to give them a hug, but didn't get up lest I lose my seat as the crowds pressed in.

I sat back and soaked in the atmosphere. Even under massive renovation—there was scaffolding all around the high altar and netting under the opening to the central tower above us—this was the place of dreams. Mass began —all in Spanish—but I understood enough of it to fully participate. The music was gorgeous, the acoustics incredible. After the eucharist—I participated again—they swung the enormous and iconic *botafumeiro*.[1] Weighing 80 kilos and standing 1.6 meters high, it swings in a tremendous arc over the transept, pulled into motion and sustained by eight men in red robes. The smoke from its incense slowly filled the air above us. A nun with a lilting soprano voice sang a hymn, the ethereal sounds resounding from the ancient stones. I thought of making a video, but didn't; I just wanted to soak in that holy moment, forever searing it into my memory. Like the day I walked into Sarria, I bookmarked the moment; it was simply beautiful. This was a great day—a *profound moment*— to be alive.

After the Mass, we walked through the cathedral, but it was packed with people. I decided to forego the traditions of visiting the statue of St. James; the line was very long and I didn't want to wait. It was now early afternoon and we decided to go for a meal with Narelle and Peter. More German pilgrims joined our group and we headed to a nearby restaurant to celebrate our accomplishment with a three-course meal and plenty of wine. After our dessert— chocolate cake—I felt more stuffed than I had in a long time. I reached down and felt my waist, realizing that I had lost two inches in the past five weeks and began to wonder if, now that I was done walking, they would come back.

After we paid our bill, and said farewell to those at our table, we headed for the Pilgrim office where we would submit our credencials one last time and receive our Compostelas. The line there was long—more than 800 pilgrims arrived that day—and we waited for two hours. Before us in line were a mother and daughter from Canada; she had walked from St.-Jean and met her mother in Leon. Behind us was a couple from Scotland who had just arrived in Santiago moments before after walking the Via de la Plata, another Camino route which comes up through central Spain. The young woman from Canada had a ukulele and led us in singing. Even though we had never met before, we felt an immediate bond because of our experi-ences. I didn't mind the wait—I had nowhere else to go that day—but was surprised to realize that of the hundreds of people in line at that moment, I didn't know *any* from my walk. When our moment came to be served, I felt another lump in my throat as the volunteer scanned my credencial and before stamping it, said, "So, you began March 29 in

St.-Jean?" "Yes," I replied. "Congratulations," she said, "That's quite an accomplishment." She asked me my name for my Compostela and after handing it to me, I asked for a second certificate, one that stated when and where I began and how far I had walked. I looked it over as she handed it to me—799 kilometers. I was curious as to why she didn't put down 800, but didn't care. It had been the walk of a lifetime.

WE STAYED in Santiago for another three days. This time, instead of feeling that restless tug to get going again, I was glad to stay put in one place. Our pensión was close to the center of the city and we were able to be at the cathedral in minutes.

The next morning, I decided to walk down to the Praza de Obradoiro to watch pilgrims enter; I loved to see the look of elation on their faces as they arrived. I walked slowly, basking in the spirit of the ancient city center and the cathedral spires which poked above them, soaking in the warm May sunshine. I paused before the northern portal again to listen to the bagpiper and pulled out my iPhone to take a video. Just then I heard a voice behind me shout, "Russ!" I turned around and saw my friend Kate, the same one who had greeted me on the Alto de Ibañeta five weeks earlier. What a surprise... She was just finishing her pilgrimage and gave me a big hug. I introduced her to Jane—who already felt like she knew her from my reports—and the three of us walked through the gate into the plaza, where she was greeted by Julie and Julia—her "girls" and several others who I recognized from along the Way. Lots of photos were taken—this is a rite of completion of the Camino, after all!

—and then we headed off together for coffee, which morphed into brunch and a long session of story-telling and laughter about our experiences. We talked of the blisters we had survived, of the long days we had endured, of the mountains we had climbed, of the wonderful people we had met. I pondered as we all shared that this was somehow a fitting book-end to the journey.

That day and the next we took our time to stroll the old city, frequently meeting scores of pilgrims that I had seen along the way: Paul and Agnes from France, Carl, from Germany, 74-year-old Peter, who informed us that he had unfortunately gotten injured and had not been able to complete the walk. There was my mentor Fred, from the U.K., and of course, Pam and Kathe, the Wisconsin Sisters, who were especially keen to meet Jane. With each one that we met, we paused and took photos, likely the last time we would be together. We said our sad farewells, but planned on keeping in touch. *Buen Camino, hermanos.*

Later, as we went through the narrow streets of Santiago, I reflected about how I had changed. I was not the same person who had ventured off from St.-Jean. I felt like I had drawn into myself the spiritual depths of the Way, the rich experiences and aspirations of those who had walked before me in recent decades and in distant centuries. Likewise, the Camino had (hopefully) drawn the best out of me, refreshed my spirit and given me inspiration for the future. I had been soaked by rain and snow, chilled to the bone, had slipped on rocky and muddy terrain. I'd been sun-burned, had endured hours of loneliness, and taken wrong turns more times than I cared to count. I'd been helped by strangers, had slept in large rooms with hundreds of snoring people, had eaten simple breakfasts, pined for cups of coffee, feasted on suppers with many, many new friends. I had learned to trust and appreciate all the good that there is in humanity. I had learned to drink in the beauty that was around me, all day, everywhere. I had learned to see God in the small subtle ways that we normally overlook.

It might just take the rest of my life to understand *every-thing* that it meant.

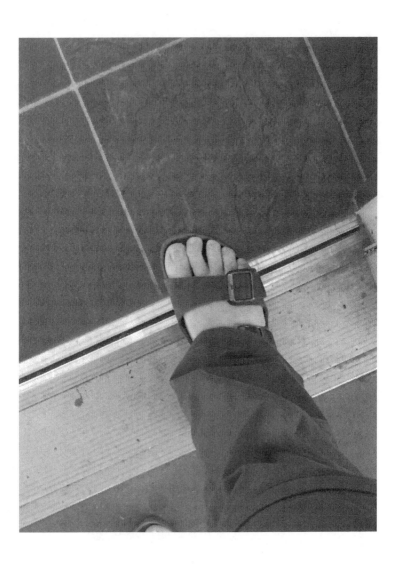

Coming Home

Swift is the step of returning
   With a heart brimming of burning
   To the door and floor that is known,
   Where the firelight brightness is shown,
   Where the loving needs no learning.

Gaelic verse of the Western Highlands

I PAUSED as I stepped over the threshold of my home: May 7, 2018, 4:43 p.m., just a day shy of six weeks since my foot last stepped over my threshold and I departed on pilgrimage. The world around me was now a rich green; the maples and the redbud trees and the wild honeysuckle undergrowth in the woods behind the house were in full-leaf, the tulips were in bloom, the mild air was balmy and delicious. The grass on the slope behind the house was long and needed to be mowed.

I was home and I was glad to be there.

I knew that walking the Camino would end. Going back to the days and weeks leading up to my adventure, even in my anticipation, I knew that there would one day be a post-Camino life. After the walk of a lifetime, I would need to come home. I had missed my family. I missed the beautiful place where I lived, the place where, after decades of moving, I finally unbundled my roots and let them sink deep. Each day begins, year-round, with a cup of coffee on my front deck, thanking God for the view, of which I never tire. Sitting there, I delight in the birds singing as they swoop from branch to branch, in the coos of the mourning doves on roofs and the lowing of the cows from the dairy farms a mile away. I delight in the scents of the woods surrounding me as they change with each season.

I also loved the Camino and the freedom of each new day. I loved the new discoveries, the fascinating people, the sense of history, the breadth of human community and culture, the expectancy of wonder or mystery around any corner. I loved the pre-dawn walks. I loved the sun rising and my shadow rising along with it, leading the way ahead of me. I loved having no agenda and no harder decision than where to stop for coffee. I loved having time for prayer, unhurried, and I loved how I felt closer to God through that.

It wasn't until I returned to the hum and motion of my "normal" daily routines and community that I realized just how hard it was going to be. Reentry is one of the greatest challenges for pilgrims, and I was no exception. I had learned a great deal about myself and I didn't want to forget any of it; I didn't want to simply return to old patterns and habits.

On my flight out of Santiago, a man sitting next to me asked me if I had "found myself" while I was walking. I paused a while before I answered. I said, "No, I don't think I was lost. But I rediscovered a great deal about myself that I had forgotten." The day after returning, I wrote this in my journal:

> I am home. Six weeks ago today, I strapped on my pack and walked out the door into a rainy morning. Now I am home from the trip of a lifetime and my life is changed forever and I pray that it stays that way... I face a new chapter in life with my soul and spirit revived, restored, renewed. I feel layers were peeled away so that the deep person within me was able to be revealed.

Medieval pilgrims *walked* home from Santiago, the return trip taking just as long as the way there. It gave them months to reflect on the experience and to adjust to the life they had lived before they left. Modern pilgrims fly home in a *day* and there is barely time to reflect on the experience before a person is thrust back into their previous life. This accounts for a saying among some experienced pilgrims that the "real Camino" begins when you return home.

An online forum for Camino pilgrims had lots of discussion about this very topic. Here is what one person said about reentry:

> Isn't it lovely, the camino life. One thing to do, one thing to deal with. Walk, eat, sleep, repeat. I long to be there every day that I'm not. The simplicity and the clarity of purpose gives us the space in our heads to deal with the other stuff. Or ignore it if we choose. There are those who live on the Camino. Their lives before led them there and the Camino gave them some comfort they had not had before. There are those of us, the 'addicts' who return again, and again, because of that special time, that special

life that the Camino gives us. What it doesn't do is remove us from the 'other' life.[1]

Another said:

I lived this most special existence, away from the materialism and chaos of this life. I learned that the most important along the Way were the non-tangible things... the camaraderie, shared wisdom, special friendships, spirituality and those funny little coincidences that would happen, or in other words, synchronicity... It was a journey of self-discovery. I discovered my own strength and courage through difficult yet very "camino moments." The Camino gives us what we need (and that can be hard sometimes). It opens the door to something very meaningful and beautiful and in its wake, we try to recreate it and we can never forget it. It's probably why so many pilgrims return again and again.[2]

Yet another questioned their old life:

Who's to say living in a house with a mortgage and a dog is how real life should be? Who is saying it isn't? I think the camino is about introducing a more simple way of life, recognizing and appreciating the simple things in life. Why can't life be more simple, like on the camino?[3]

One person said that they were a "stranger in their own life," while another said that they didn't "fit into the puzzle of their life" any longer.

I had many of the same sentiments after I returned, but my first several months back were busy ones: I attended my youngest son's junior college graduation; helped another son with home remodeling and helped yet a third who was moving home with his family after five years overseas. I went with a friend on a "bucket list" adventure, cycling the length of the UK, from Lands End in Cornwall to John O' Groats in Scotland, a 1,000-mile trip.

During this time, I continued to grapple with understanding the meaning of my pilgrimage. I had an inner restlessness that I knew couldn't be simply cured by going back to Spain and doing it all again, as some people have done. As much as I have the itch to wander, I am anchored to my home, to my family, and I can't and don't want to leave.

So, I decided to write a book.

Before I left for Spain, I was asked if I was going to write a book about my pilgrimage. "No," I said, "I'm just going to walk it, the experience is enough." Along the Camino, when I told fellow pilgrims that I was a book publisher, and wanted to become a writer, some said, "Oh, a writer. Are you going to write a book about your walk?" I truthfully replied, "Not likely." Even shortly after arriving home, I was asked by friends, "Are you going to write a book about the Camino?" Again, I replied, "I doubt it."

Yet while I was in Spain with many hours alone, the Camino was working on me, and my inner life opened up; that was what I wanted. As it opened up, writing began to spill out, first in my head and eventually in the form of letters, postcards, emails, a journal and some posts on Facebook. That was all very satisfying, but I still had no intention of writing a book.

I was out on a bike ride one afternoon a few weeks after returning, when the inspiration for this book came to me. It was simple, like a yellow arrow on the wall, pointing to the path. Even though I'd published for hundreds of authors in my life, even though I knew and loved the publishing business, a book seemed beyond the scope of both my attention span and my ambitions. Yet, the idea was obvious: I was planning on doing more writing myself and on starting a self-publishing business, so why not start with a book of my own? Just as I learned to be attentive on the Camino, I learned to be attentive once I came home and, starting with that moment of inspiration during the bike ride, the arrows all pointed in the direction of a book.

A few months later I gathered together all the bits of what I had written in journals, letters and online postings, all my stories, my impressions and thoughts. Over the summer I had given presentations about my experience and those talks provided more material. Talking about it relit the fire inside. I read books by other pilgrims. I reviewed the thousands of photos I had taken; they helped preserve the memories of the entire journey, village by village, kilometer by kilometer. Everything I had written, all of those memories and experiences formed the kernels of chapters, and then I spaced them all out along the road, from St.-Jean to Santiago.

This book became my way of making sense of my experience and of integrating it into my "normal life" at home. It's the way I keep it alive in my spirit, the way I continue the journey. As a wise hospitalero in Logroño said to us during our communal supper, "Once you have walked the Camino, you will walk it every day for the rest of your life."

Afterword: Better to Die with
Your Memories

The compact between writing and walking is almost as old as literature—a walk is only a step away from a story and every path tells.

Robert McFarlane, *The Old Ways.*

A year has passed since I stepped across the threshold of my house, the start of my pilgrimage. A year has passed since I entered the western plaza of the Cathedral in Santiago and realized to my astonishment that I had made it: 500 miles, my dream—the walk of a lifetime.

While the experience slowly recedes in the rear-view mirror of my life, I still think back vividly to those two moments and the hair stands up on my arms. Tears well up in the corners of my eyes. They are among life's seminal moments, and there were many more moments along the Way. And people. And vistas…

I wrote this book because I had to follow the signs; I wrote this book to keep the memories alive. I wrote this book to understand what my pilgrimage meant. I wrote this book to inspire others. I'm an advocate for walking and cycling, an evangelist for them both, but I'm also an advocate for *dreaming*. Life is too short, too precious, not to live your dreams and you are never too old to live them, either. I saw these words painted on a stone in Galicia: *Better to die with your memories than your dreams*. I was fortunate at 61 to have had the health, encouragement and adventuresome spirit to fulfill a dream.

The meaning of my journey has deepened each day in the last year. I'd like to distill its meaning more, let it sit longer, before I publish it. I could spend more time with the story: I could polish it, refine it, improve it. I have frequently agonized over its creation: writing, re-writing, deleting, starting over. (It reminded me of my tendency to over-prepare for the Camino.) But just like the Camino, it has to have an ending, and so this is the time to let it go, to release it. All books have to end, and so does this one.

The experience will continue to reveal new meaning in my life; so be it. I hope to walk the Camino Frances again, God-willing; and that journey will have its own meaning. I hope to do it with members of my family. There will be more stamps on a new credential, new pilgrims to meet, new hardships, new adventures, new stories. There will be other paths to walk, too, and more stories to tell of them.

"He heard the strange call that, for centuries, has seen so many humans become their best selves, inhabiting that sacred space that is the Camino de Santiago."[1]

Now, I belong to the journey.
Buen Camino, hermanos.

My walking stages

Day -2: March 27: Harrisonburg to Dulles Airport and United Airlines flight to Paris.
Day -1: Landed in Paris, took train and bus to St.-Jean
Day 1: St.-Jean to Roncesvalles (24k, March 29)
Day 2: Roncesvalles to Zubiri (22.3k, March 30)
Day 3: Zubiri to Pamplona (21.1k, March 31)
Day 4: Pamplona to Puenta La Reina (23.8 April 1)
Day 5: Puenta La Reina to Estella (21.8k, April 2)
Day 6: Estella to Los Arcos (21.6k, April 3)
Day 7: Los Arcos to Logroño (27.6k, April 4)
Day 8: Logroño to Najera (29.6k, April 5)
Day 9: Najera to Grañon (28.1k, April 6)
Day 10: Grañon to Tosantos (20.6k, April 7)
Day 11: Tosantos to Atapuerca (25.3k, April 8)
Day 12: Atapuerca to Burgos (19.8k, April 9)
Rest day in Burgos (April 10)
Day 13: Burgos to Hontanas (31.4, April 11)
Day 14: Hontanos to Boadilla (28.5k, April 12)
Day 15: Boadilla to Carrion (24.5k, April 13)
Day 16: Carrion to Terradillos (26.6k, April 14)

Day 17: Terradillos to Calzadilla (26.4k, April 15)
Day 18: Calzadilla to Mansilla de las Mulas (23.6k, April 16)
Day 19: Mansilla to Leon (17.9k, April 17)
Day 20: Leon to San Martín del Camino (25.2k, April 18)
Day 21: San Martin to Astorga (23.9k, April 19)
Day 22: Astorga to Rabanal (20.5k, April 20)
Day 23: Rabanal to Molinaseca (24.9k, April 21)
Day 24: Molinaseca to Pieros (25.5k, April 22)
Day 25: Pieros to Trabadelo (16.2k, April 23)
Day 26: Trabadelo to Liñares (21.7k, April 24)
Day 27: Liñares to Triacastela (17.7k, April 25)
Day 28: Triacastela to Sarria (18.7k, April 26)
Rest day in Sarria (April 27)
Day 29 Sarria to Portomarin (22k, April 28)
Day 30: Portomarin to Portos (19.8k, April 29)
Day 31: Portos to Melide (20.4k, April 30)
Day 32: Melide to Salceda (24.7k, May 1)
Day 33: Salceda to Lavacolla (18.3k, May 2)
Day 34: Lavacolla to Santiago (10k, May 3)

Notes

1. Whispers of the Camino

1. "James" is Iago in Spanish, so *Santiago* literally means "Saint James." *Compostela* can mean either "field of stars" (compost + stella) but could also mean "cemetery." It is the place where St. James' bones were buried and shepherds located them because they saw stars dancing over the field, so the word could really have either meaning.

2. *The Canterbury Tales*, written in the 14th century, is a classic of Middle-English writing that many of us had to slog through in high school English. Canterbury was the most popular pilgrimage in England, but local pilgrimages were common and there were literally hundreds of such sites in England and the rest of Europe.

3. I abandoned thinking in miles when I walked the Camino, since everything—the signposts and my guidebooks—was in kilometers. A kilometer is .6 miles. Twenty-five kilometers is 15 miles.

4. The earliest guidebook for pilgrims was among the five books in the *Codex Calixtinus*, written and circulated in the 12th century.

5. *Peregrino* is Spanish for pilgrim. In French they are called *Pèlerins*.

6. The word "way" can be the same as "camino" in Spanish and I often refer to the Camino as the "Way." In English this is a word with rich meaning: it can be a route, a road, a path, an artery, a trail; it also has broader meanings that can be spiritual, connoting a pattern of life. The early Christians in the first centuries were originally called followers of The Way.

7. The same Celts who dominated all of northern Europe, including the U.K. and Ireland, came to Northern Spain over 2,500 years ago. The rainy northwestern region of Spain, where Santiago de Compostela is located, is called Galicia and its culture still carries Celtic influence in foods, music, language and architecture.

8. *Calzada* is best translated something like "highway," which is what the old Roman roads were. Many towns along the Camino Frances are named with *Calzada*.

9. An *albergue*, also called a *refugio*, is a hostel for pilgrims. Located every few kilometers, they offer an affordable place to stay, typically with a warm shower, bunk bed and kitchen or restaurant. Some operate by donation. A pilgrim must present a credential in order to stay in one. In the middle ages they were called *hospitals* or places of hospitality.

10. In 2018, the year I walked it, 327,378 pilgrims were issued *Compostelas* in Santiago, the largest number in modern history. A pilgrim needs to complete at least the last 100 kilometers to receive a Compestela. About ten percent of those who receive Compostelas walk the entire 800 kilometers from St.-Jean-Pied-de-Port.

11. There are two routes over the Pyrenees, more or less equal in distance, from St.-Jean to Roncesvalles. The more remote or "Napoleon Route" climbs to 1,500 meters before descending to Roncesvalles. It was developed during the Middle Ages since the lower and easier "Valcarlos Route" (which I took) was prone to bandits. The week before I went, two Scots had to be rescued off the top of the Napoleon route after getting stuck in three feet of snow.

12. David co-authored the *Camino de Santiago* guidebook (Village to Village Press), with his wife, Anna Dintaman. I used it the entire way.

13. In the Middle Ages, it was customary for pilgrims to go before their church and announce their intention to make a pilgrimage and received a blessing and prayer for their journey.

2. Following the Signs

1. Pilgrims are almost always asked to remove their hiking shoes or boots at the entrance to an albergue. With hundreds passing through every week, this helps keep it clean.

2. Back in Chapter 1 I had mentioned that there are two ways one can cross the Pyrenees between St.-Jean and Roncesvalles, the lower, Valcarlos route and the higher and more remote and scenic Napoleon route. Both are roughly the same distance, but the Napoleon route is "officially" closed from November to April.

3. Can you Help Me Find My Girls?

1. In 778, the Frankish Emperor Charlemagne was heading northward over these mountains, after six years battling Muslims in Spain. His nephew Roland was in charge of the rear guard, and as they crossed the Pyrenees, the rear guard was ambushed. Roland died in the battle and Charlemagne supposedly had his body buried at the top of the Alto de Ibañeta, hence the location of the monument.

2. A *hospitalero* is a volunteer in an *albergue*, and typically one who has previously walked the Camino themselves.

3. The word hospice is a delightful word, and includes some of the most important human values and practices: welcoming, caring, and graciously giving to, and receiving from, each other. It comes to us via Old French from the Latin root, *hospit*, meaning "guest, host, stranger."

From it we derive many English words, including host, hostess, hospital, hospitality, hospitable, hospice, hosteler, hostel, hotel.

4. In many of the older towns along the Camino Frances there are evening services in churches, usually a Catholic Mass, where they conclude with a blessing of pilgrims. When not too tired in the evenings, I tried to go to these. They were typically in Spanish, but even though I wasn't Catholic and couldn't understand much of the language, I enjoyed them anyway and always came away uplifted.

4. Apparently, I Walk

1. Boers, Arthur Paul, *The Way is Made by Walking.*
2. I find that walking as a response to personal crisis is a common theme. It was true among many of those I met along the Camino, and in many of the newer books that are written about "Camino experiences." I was walking because I knew I wanted to change my life, perhaps *before* I encountered a crisis.
3. National Geographic Society, 2008.

6. Encountering the Magic

1. I had not yet gotten used to the Spanish coffee machines, which in reality were better than in the U.S., pouring espressos in various combinations of milk and sugar—or without, as in *"sin azur."*
2. Many veteran Camino walkers and writers refer to "The Camino Magic." It may mean something slightly different to each person, but it commonly refers to unexpected experiences and encounters, rare in everyday life, but frequent on the Camino. Some pilgrims refer to it as "synchronicity" or an amazing alignment of events. It is probably the thing that everyone misses the most when they return to "normal life."

7. The Camino is a River

1. A *porrón* is a glass wine pitcher with a long spout.
2. A retablo literally means, "behind the altar," and refers to elaborate and even ornate theatrical scenes, including decorated statuary, often in gold. They often fill the entire space behind the altars in nearly every Spanish church.
3. Luke 6:38, *New International Version*
4. Day, Dorothy, *The Long Loneliness,* p. 285.

8. Feet, Shoes and Mud

1. San Juan de Ortgega is now known as the patron saint of innkeepers, and curiously, also of fertility.
2. This bus ride to the shopping center was the only time in April that I took any motorized transport, probably the only time in my life that I didn't ride in a car for an entire month.
3. I only wore them about twice after that; I had passed the worst of the weather.

9. We Pack our Fears

1. Ashmore, Jean-Christie, *To Walk Far, Carry Less*.
2. While ten percent of body weight is most commonly suggested load for pilgrims. Those walking in warmer weather—May to September—are able to get by with less.
3. Sony RX-100 M3, f 1.8, 24-70mm lens, 1" sensor. I noticed that most people just use their smartphones for photos.
4. Gitlitz, David, and Davidson, Linda Kay, *The Pilgrimage Road to Santiago*. This is really the most comprehensive guide to the history, culture, flora, fauna and geography of the Camino. It is available as an eBook, but since I was trying to get away from using my phone, I chose to carry a used paperback copy that I bought online. Even as heavy as it was, I never regretted carrying it.
5. Walking long distances is actually the most effective way to lose weight.
6. Thoreau, Henry David, *Walden* p. 76.
7. Americans regularly consume more than anyone else, per capita, on the planet; we used 6 times as much energy as someone in Mexico, 38 times as much as a person in India and 531 times as much as the average person in Ethiopia. See: McKibben, Bill, *Deep Economy*, p. 184.
8. I recommend *Minimalism* and *Everything That Remains* by Josh Fields Millburn and Ryan Nicodemus, aka "The Minimalists" who can be found online at theminimalists.com.
9. Matthew 6:19-21. It is significant to note that Jesus talked about simplicity, money and possessions more than any other moral topic, though one would strain hard to find that in modern American church life.

10. Solitude

1. Chittister, Joan, *The Gift of Years*, pp. 145-146
2. Gabarain, Antxon Gonzáles, *The Great Western Walk*, p. 332.

3. Acts 2:44, 46, "All the believers were together and had everything in common. Selling their possessions and goods, they gave to anyone as he had need... They broke bread in their homes and ate together with glad and sincere hearts."

    Acts 4:32, "All the believers were one in heart and mind. No one claimed that any of his possessions was his own, but they shared everything they had.

4. Daily "offices" refer to fixed times of prayer, traditionally liturgical, which came to Christianity by inheritance from Judaism. For many it refers to fixed prayers that move through the day. For monastics, that can be up to seven times a day. Like many individuals, I have adapted elements of these prayers to fit my own time of individual prayer each morning, and mine is especially influenced by the Celtic tradition. With some adaptations, this prayer is from David Adam's book, *The Road of Life: Reflections on Searching and Longing,* pp. 134-35.

5. "The watches of the night" is usually around 3:00 a.m. and was typical in all cultures before the advent of the lightbulb, which artificially extended the day.

6. Chitister, *op. cit.*, p. 146.

7. Much of that original thought and writing eventually became part of this book.

11. I'm not in a hurry

1. Ortberg, John, *The Life You've Always Wanted.* He is quoting Meyer Friedman.

2. Thoreau, Henry David, *Walden,* p. 105.

14. Receiving the Camino

1. There is more than one Villafranca along the Camino Frances, and it literally means, "The village of the Franks," but "franca" more likely means "foreigner." People from all over Medieval Europe settled along the Camino and this village was one of those places. Always an important town along the Camino Frances, by the mid-12th century half of the population was indeed foreign. The Fenix albergue itself continues this history. Begun in the 1980's by Jesus Jato, in plastic tents, it endured fires, before being rebuilt or "reborn" (hence Phoenix) in stone. Communal meals and warm and enthusiastic hosts continue the ancient spirit of hospitality there.

16. Walking two moons

1. The term "touragrinos" or "touristagrinos" is often used to describe the tourist-peregrino.
2. Portomarín was an ancient town with a Roman bridge over the river Miño. In 1956 the river was dammed and the entire town was relocated stone-by-stone to a nearby hill. When the reservoir is low, the ancient bridge can still be seen.

17. You did it!

1. The botafumeiro is not swung at every pilgrim mass, but only on certain days or for large tour groups who are willing to pay several hundred euros.

18. Coming Home

1. Tincatiner, Moderator, www.Caminodesantiago.me.
2. Anonymous, Camino de Santiago forum, www.caminodesantiago.me.
3. Spencer-Milan, Kate, www.caminodesantiago.me.

Afterword: Better to Die with Your Memories

1. De la Riera, Jose Antonio, from the Introduction to *The Great Western Walk*.

Additional sources

Chapter 15: "A Conversation with Artist Makoto Fujimura on Beauty, Mission, and Culture Care," IMB online, https://www.imb.org/2017/09/25/conversation-artist-makoto-fujimura-beauty-mission-culture-care/

Chapter 17: Kavafis, Konstandinos, *I will walk towards my Ithaka,* this is the last stanza of a poem cited in numerous books and online. See: http://www.kavafis.eu/poems.htm

(Photo opposite is Kate and her "girls" in Santiago)

Bibliography of Sources, annotated

Adam, David, *The Road of Life: Reflections on Searching and Longing.* Harrisburg: Morehouse, 2004. I am indebted to David for many wonderful prayers he has written in the Celtic tradition, including one I adapted and called my "pilgrim's prayer."

Ashmore, Jean-Christie, *To Walk Far, Carry Less.* Walk Far Media, 2011. A good primer on what to pack for a Camino and what to expect along the way.

Avia, Elyn, *Following the Milky Way: A Pilgrimage on the Camino de Santiago.* Boulder: Pilgrims' Process 2001. A very early memoir of a pilgrimage on the Camino, from 1982

Boers, Arthur Paul, *The Way is Made by Walking.* Downers Grove: IVP Books, 2007.

Chittister, Joan, *The Gift of Years.* New York: Bluebridge, 2008.

Codd, Kevin A., *To the Field of Stars: A Pilgrim's Journey to Santiago de Compostela.* Grand Rapids: Wm. B. Eerdmans 2008.

Day, Dorothy, *The Long Loneliness.* New York: Harper Collins, 1952.

Dintamin, Anna, and Landis, David, *Camino de Santiago, Village to Village Guide.* Harrisonburg: Village to Village Press, 2017. This is the guidebook that I carried with me on my journey and I found it indispensable. Also available now in a version with maps only and also in eBook.

Francis, John, *Planetwalker.* Washington D.C. National Geographic 2008.

Gabarain, Antxon Gonzalez, *The Great Westward Walk: From the Front Door to the End of the Earth.* Translated by Rebekah Scott. Spanish version, *El Gran Caminante,* 2013. My favorite memoir of a pilgrim.

Gitlitz, David and Davidson, Linda Kay, *The Pilgrimage Road to Santiago: The Complete Cultural Handbook.* New York: St. Martin's Griffin, 2000. The most complete guide to culture, history and geography of the Camino Frances.

Jenkins, Peter, *A Walk Across America.* Old Tappan: Fleming H. Revell, 1979.

Lee, Laurie, *As I Walked Out One Midsummer Morning.* Middlesex: Penguin Books, 1969. A delightfully written memoir of a young Englishman's journey across pre-Civil War Spain.

McLean, G.R.D., *Celtic Spiritual Verse.* London: SPCK, 2002.

McKibben, Bill, *Deep Economy.* New York: Times Books, 2007.

McFarlane, Robert, *The Old Ways.* New York: Penguin Group, 2012.

Melczer, William, *The Pilgrim's Guide to Santiago de Compostela.* New York: Italica Press 1993. This book contains a translation of Book Five of the *Codex Calixtinus,* an early Medieval guide to the Camino de Santiago.

Newcomer, Carrie, *the beautiful not yet,* Available Light 2016.

Thoreau, Henry David, *Walden.* Boston: Beacon Press 1997.

_____, *Walking.* Bedford: Applewood Books.

Tozer, A.W., *The Pursuit of God.* Camp Hill: Christian Publications, 1982.

Acknowledgments

To all the Camino friends and acquaintances that I made along the way: Raymond, Paul and Lauri, Sandro and Cynthia, Kate, Julie and Julia, William, Patrick, Pam, Kathe, George, Pauline, Bobby, Alan and Terry, Miri, Narelle and Peter, who shared meals, coffee, laundry, chocolate or conversations during long stretches of the road; thank you for your companionship.

To the anonymous hospitaleros, especially volunteers, who lent encouragement, shouldered my pack at the end of the day, made me laugh, gave me a cup of coffee, or just gave a welcome word of advice, thank you. You give the Camino part of the magic that ordinary life should have.

To my wife, Jane, who encouraged me to stick with the writing, thank you. You are always my first and best reader, editor and critic, besides being my beloved life-companion and trekking partner.

To my daughters Carolyn and Allison, who read and marked up my manuscript like the great English teachers that you are, thank you. The apple did not fall far from the tree.

To my sons, Nathan, Giles and Andre, thank you for the excellent advice on design.

To my son Francis and his wife Julia, thank you for the poles. They were the angels that kept my feet from slipping.

To my editors, Saloma Miller Furlong and Susan Lahey, thank you for ironing out the wrinkles in my prose, for pointing out the redundancies, backward clauses and confusing terms or syntax. You have made me a better writer.

I wrote much of this book at Shenandoah Joe's in Harrisonburg. Thanks to the baristas there for the good cups of coffee: dark roast, in a mug, with room.

Café con leche in Salceda, the town that forgot to be unhappy.

PILGRIM PATHS *to* ASSISI

300 MILES *on the* WAY OF SAINT FRANCIS

RUSS EANES

About the Author

Russ Eanes is a writer, walker and cyclist from Harrisonburg, Virginia, where he lives with his wife, three of his adult children and five of his seven grandchildren. He also enjoys traveling, gardening, reading and photography. In 2018 he "downshifted" to experience a less hectic pace of life and is now putting to use several decades' experience in the publishing business to work as an editor, publishing coach and consultant. This is his first book.

What did Russ do next, if walking the Camino de Santiago was "The Walk of a Lifetime?" He and his wife kept going, by walking the Way of Saint Francis, between Florence and Italy. Those who enjoyed *The Walk of a Lifetime* will appreciate this next walking adventure *Pilgrim Paths to Assisi: 300 Miles on the Way of St. Francis* (opposite). Told in the same lively and personal narrative, the story is full of challenging mountain climbs, history, Italian cuisine, row after row of olive groves and vineyards, and above all with tales of history's most beloved saint, Francis of Assisi.

Made in United States
Orlando, FL
07 July 2023

34812428R00124